Breaking 300

The Secrets to a Powerful Golf Swing

By Fil Falcon

COPYRIGHT

Visit publishers website
www.LondonLeafPublishing.com

Visit authors website
www.FilFalcon.com

Visit online golf lessons
www.Breaking300.com

DEDICATION

I want to dedicate this book to my wife Jessica and my family. I have been working on this book for several years. Along the way my family has patiently been supportive of my many projects. I have the best family a man could ask for. I love you all.

DISCLAIMER

Before you begin any exercise program and follow any of the advice, instructions, or recommendations in this book, you should first consult with your doctor and have a physical examination. The recommendations, instructions and advice contained within this book are offered for informational purposes only and are in no way intended to replace or to be construed as medical advice.

London Leaf Publishing LLC, the author Fil Falcon and Breaking 300 offer no warranties, guarantees or representations regarding the advice, instructions, advice or any other information contained in this book.

London Leaf Publishing LLC, the author Fil Falcon and Breaking 300 and their respective agents, heirs, assigns, contractors, and employees shall not be liable for any claims, demands, damages, rights of action or causes of action, present or future, arising out of or connected to the use of any of the information contained in this book, including any injuries resulting there from.

CONTENTS

INTRODUCTION..11

CHAPTER 1...13

ATTACK ANGLE...15

POSITIVE ATTACK ANGLE DISADVANTAGES.......................21

MOI...22

GEAR EFFECT...24

SMASH FACTOR..27

SWEET SPOT..29

CLIMATE EFFECT..32

CHAPTER 2...35

LOWER BACK STRETCH...36

HULA HOOP STRETCH...37

SITTING HIP & BACK STRETCH..38

LEANING HIP & BACK STRETCH.......................................39

HAMSTRING & CALF STRETCH...40

ARM CIRCLE STRETCH..41

3 CLUB STRETCH..42

CHAPTER 3...45

POWER GRIP...46

POWER GRIP PRESSURE..50

POWER COIL...51

POWER PIVOT...54

POWER BACKSWING...56

POWER HINGE..58

CHAPTER 4 61

Impact Zone 62

Wider TakeAway 64

Swoosh Drill 66

Throw The Ball Drill 69

Downswing Sequence 71

CHAPTER 5 75

Forearm Strength - Stress Ball 76

Shoulder Strength – Rotator Cuff 77

Core Strength – Obliques 79

Lower Back Strength - Superman 81

Hip & Leg Strength – Lunge & Twist 82

Hip Strength – Hip Rotation 83

CHAPTER 6 85

The Grip 86

The Shaft 87

The Clubhead 89

Technology 91

Loft 92

Golf Balls 93

FINAL WORDS 95

INTRODUCTION

Breaking 300 yards off the tee box is an achievable milestone for the average golfer. In this book I reveal several simple ways to improve your clubhead speed resulting in longer drives down the center of the fairway. I spent a major part of my life developing a golf swing that allows me to break 300 yards with the driver. Regardless of your swing type, handicap, or skill level this book is designed to help every golfer improve overall distance and move one step closer to breaking 300.

The focus of this book is to build a sturdy foundation for your golf swing. If you have a good, solid foundation, the rest of the swing will naturally fall into place. The majority of golfers have a good idea about how to hit the ball, but their foundation may not be the strongest. As a result, they are forced to use their athleticism to compensate for swing faults. By building a stronger foundation from the beginning, you will have more fun and see increased distance in your golf game.

Thank you for sharing my interest in breaking 300 yards off the tee box. I wish you the best of luck in discovering the hidden distance within your reach.

CHAPTER 1

THE SCIENCE OF DISTANCE

Strength, speed and technique are all vital components of hitting the golf ball 300 yards down the fairway, but there are a few other essentials that you may be missing when attempting to achieve this goal. There is also a lot of science and technology behind maximizing the overall distance. Over the decades, there have been tremendous strides in the development of technology as it relates to golf. The best improvements with technology come from the golf ball, driver, shaft and custom fitting. There seems to be a new golf ball coming out every year and a driver that is designed to go along with it. New and improved shafts that are just a bit better than their former models are hitting the market every year. Every year golf companies manage to discover new revolutionary breakthroughs in design and race to release products to the market so players can benefit. To maximize your distance off the tee, it is essential to take advantage of this new technology as it is being introduced to the public. I am not necessarily saying that you must go out and buy the latest and greatest equipment every year like the tour pros have. The truth is, most tour pros get the majority of their equipment for free and get paid to play certain brands that sponsor them. Unless you have the cash flow to purchase and get fitted every year for new equipment, focus on making the right equipment purchases rather than the most trendy ones. Thanks to technology, you can improve your game without making big improvements in your actual swing or technique. In the quest to improve your overall distance it would be wise to understand how the science of golf really works and how you can benefit from it. In this chapter I will briefly explain the science of distance and how it directly affects your game.

ATTACK ANGLE

Even with your current swing speed you can hit the ball further right now. All you have to do is figure out how to optimize the attack angle with the loft of your driver. Below is a series of TrackMan charts representing club fitting data to optimize your driver distance. TrackMan has made revolutionary discoveries using state of the art radar technology to determine many aspects of ball flight. These charts represent a study conducted with vigorous testing of many different club speeds to optimize your overall carry and total yardage with the driver. Once you spot your current club head speed, you will notice that the attack angle of 5 has overall more yardage than attack angles of -5 and 0. What does this mean? This data is essentially telling us most people will benefit from hitting the ball on an upswing rather than a downswing to increase overall distance with the driver. To maximize distance you need to minimize your overall spin rate. The ball has been proven to travel further and faster through the air if it has less spin. There is a limit however, you need enough spin to make the ball stay in the air long enough to maximize distance depending on the conditions and golf courses you play in. Otherwise, without enough spin, the ball will hit the ground too soon and roll, losing precious distance off the tee.

The majority of golfers hit their driver like they hit their irons, down on the ball with a descending blow. In reality, if they want to hit the ball further without a drastic swing change they should hit the driver with a positive attack angle. The driver is the only club in the bag that you want to hit using an upswing. Why? Have you ever tried to hit a driver off the grass without using a tee? It is very difficult to make the ball airborne unless you have a high swing speed and hit the ball flush. The reason you want a positive attack angle on the ball with the driver is because it creates less spin. The driver is also the least lofted club in the bag and therefore the hardest one to hit straight. The second reason you want to hit the driver on an upswing is because of the size of the clubhead. These days the drivers are huge compared to the old wooden heads and they require taller tees in order to be hit properly. The taller tees are easier to hit, and will help you learn how to hit the ball on the upswing much faster.

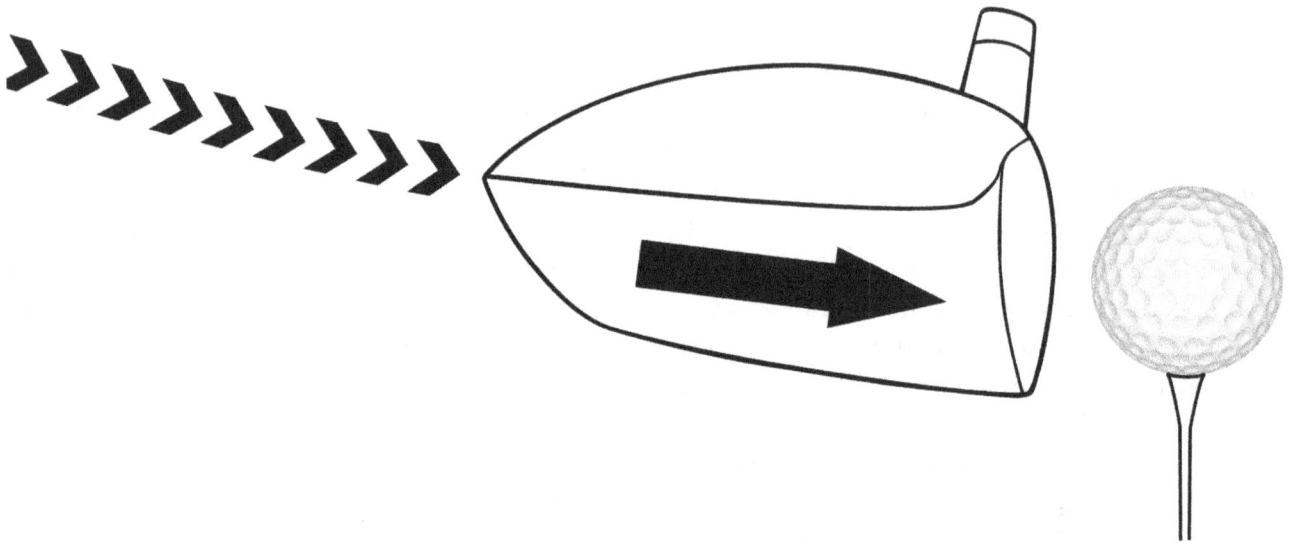

Downward (Negative) Attack Angle

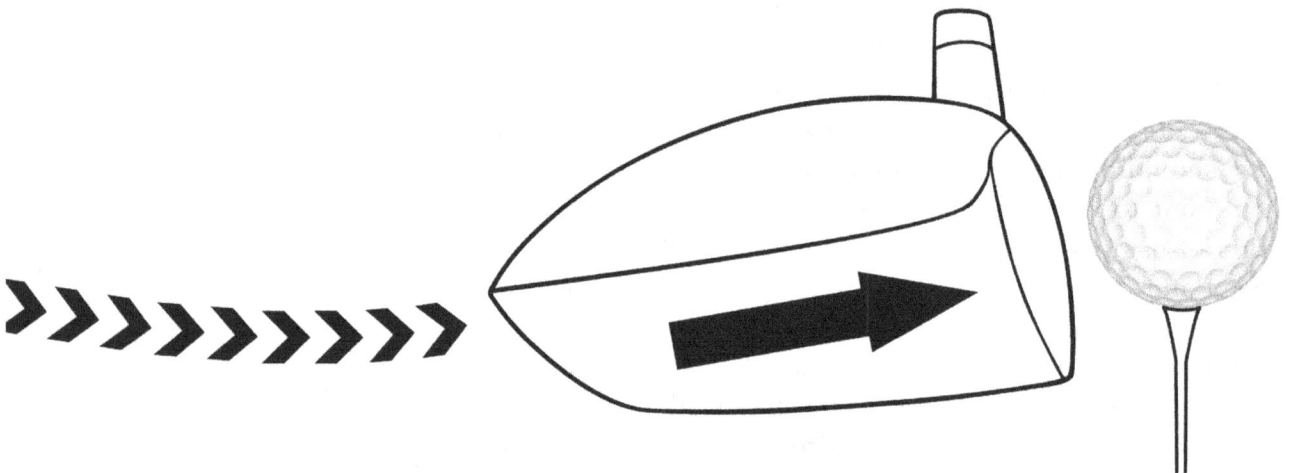

Upward (Positive) Attack Angle

The driver charts below start with a swing speed of 75 mph and end at 120 mph. If your swing speed is higher than 120 mph, congratulations you are gifted. If you are like the rest of us and fall within the 75 – 120 mph you are in luck.. TrackMan has run countless tests and found a way to optimize swing speeds that will benefit your carry and total carry from the tee box using the driver. The main discovery: attack angles with an upswing on clubhead impact generate less spin, higher ball speed and increased yardage. As a result the ball travels much further without a change in swing speed.

There are two types of charts here. One is for optimizing your carry and the other is for total yards. This can be very useful depending on the golf course and conditions you normally play in.

If you live in a very wet climate where it rains often, you will be looking to optimize your overall carry. Since the golf ball doesn't have much roll in wet and soggy grass, you want to have the carry do most of the work for you. On the other hand if the conditions call for a hot climate with very hard and bouncy fairway, you want to optimize your total yards. That way you can take advantage of the roll.

To take full advantage of these charts, I would recommend getting fitted by your local professional. Don't just go to any professional. If you are serious about improving your distance you need to find a club fitter that is using the latest technology. Ask the fitter what kind of equipment they are using and if they have a TrackMan Launch Monitor. They are the leading brand in launch monitor technology and nobody else comes close. If the fitter is using TrackMan technology they will be able to more precisely determine how to optimize your distance. Those exact measurements will play a vital role in increasing your overall drive distance. Don't be afraid to print the optimizer charts and compare the numbers to your own readings. The charts can be very helpful tools in your pursuit of breaking 300 yards.

CARRY YARD OPTIMIZER CHART BY TRACKMAN

Club Speed (mph)	Attack Angle (deg)	Ball Speed (mph)	Launch Angle (deg)	Spin Rate (rpm)	Carry (yards)	Total (yards)	Dynamic Loft (deg)
75	-5	104	14.6	3722	143	166	18.2
	0	107	16.3	3121	154	178	19.2
	5	108	19.2	2720	164	187	21.8
80	-5	113	12.9	3652	160	176	16.2
	0	115	15.5	3179	171	187	18.3
	5	116	18.0	2648	181	197	20.3
85	-5	121	11.9	3669	175	199	15.0
	0	123	14.5	3164	187	211	17.1
	5	124	17.0	2596	197	223	19.1
90	-5	129	11.1	3689	191	215	14.0
	0	131	13.4	3093	203	228	15.8
	5	132	16.4	2633	214	239	18.5
95	-5	137	9.9	3626	207	243	12.6
	0	138	12.7	3114	219	244	15.0
	5	140	15.7	2595	231	256	17.6
100	-5	144	9.6	3722	222	244	12.2
	0	146	12.1	3118	235	272	14.3
	5	148	14.9	2538	247	272	16.7
105	-5	152	8.7	3675	237	260	11.1
	0	154	11.2	3038	251	275	13.2
	5	155	14.5	2563	263	288	16.2
110	-5	160	7.7	3570	252	275	9.9
	0	162	10.5	2970	266	291	12.3
	5	163	13.7	2435	279	305	15.2
115	-5	168	7.0	3548	266	290	9.2
	0	170	9.8	2919	281	306	11.6
	5	171	13.0	2358	295	321	14.4
120	-5	176	6.1	3433	281	305	8.1
	0	178	9.3	2890	296	321	11.0
	5	179	12.6	2343	310	350	14.0

TOTAL YARD OPTIMIZER CHART BY TRACKMAN

Club Speed (mph)	Attack Angle (deg)	Ball Speed (mph)	Launch Angle (deg)	Spin Rate (rpm)	Carry (yards)	Total (yards)	Dynamic Loft (deg)
75	-5	107	11.8	3214	140	182	14.9
	0	109	13.0	2506	147	195	15.3
	5	11	15.3	1976	156	206	17.1
80	-5	115	10.1	3078	154	188	12.8
	0	117	12.1	2494	163	199	14.3
	5	118	14.8	2005	174	209	16.5
85	-5	123	9.3	3110	169	215	11.9
	0	125	11.7	2568	180	228	13.8
	5	126	14.0	1964	189	241	15.6
90	-5	131	8.5	3122	185	231	11.0
	0	132	10.8	2517	196	245	12.8
	5	134	13.8	2021	207	259	15.3
95	-5	138	7.9	3144	201	247	10.2
	0	140	10.5	2565	213	262	12.3
	5	141	13.0	1948	223	276	14.4
100	-5	146	7.2	3118	216	262	9.3
	0	148	10.0	2570	230	278	11.7
	5	149	12.4	1887	239	293	13.7
105	-5	154	6.4	3071	231	278	8.4
	0	156	9.1	2461	243	294	10.7
	5	157	11.7	1810	254	309	12.9
110	-5	162	5.6	3005	245	293	7.5
	0	163	8.7	2471	260	310	10.2
	5	165	11.1	1716	268	326	12.2
115	-5	170	5.3	3030	261	307	7.1
	0	171	8.0	2396	274	325	9.5
	5	172	10.7	1681	285	342	11.7
120	-5	178	4.5	2929	273	322	6.2
	0	179	7.7	2382	290	340	9.0
	5	180	10.3	1636	300	358	11.3

After you have found your swing speed, the first thing you will notice is the huge difference in distance between the downward attack angle of -5 and the upward attack angle of +5. This is a big deal for anyone who wants to drive the ball further. Imagine all you have to do is swing up on the ball rather than swinging down on the ball. Let's take a look at the numbers. If your drivers swing speed is 100 mph and you have always hit down on the ball with an attack angle of -5, your total yard optimizer distance would be 262. After making a tiny adjustment to your swing, you start swinging up on the ball and manage to hit the ball with an attack angle of +5. Your overall yard optimizer distance would be 293. That is a 31 yard improvement. Using the same swing speed you managed to hit it 31 yards further just by hitting up on the ball. This demonstrates the importance of swinging up on the ball and getting fitted for the proper driver and shaft using the latest launch monitor technology. The club fitters can easily get you into the proper launch angles and spin rates to optimize your overall distance. There are thousands of shafts on the market, each one designed for a specific ball flight. There are many different types of driver that have different reactions. All you have to do is try them out and see what works for you. It's very easy to gain yards, you just need a little push in the right direction. After making the adjustments necessary to hit up on the ball, the next step is to increase your clubhead speed and better your technique. A small swing improvement and combined with strengthening exercises will get you one step closer to achieving your goal of driving 300 yards.

Chart Glossary

Club Speed – measures the speed in miles per hour when the club head makes center impact with the ball.

Attack Angle – measured in degrees, the vertical angle of impact the clubhead makes with the ball. Upward angle of attack or hitting up on the ball has a positive degree. Downward angle of attack or hitting down on the ball has a negative degree.

Ball Speed – measures the speed in miles per hour the ball makes directly after impact with the clubface.

Launch Angle – measured in degrees, the initial angle the ball is launched with relation to the ground.

Spin Rate – measured in revolutions (rotations) per minute, amount of times a ball will fully turn during the ball flight.

Carry – measured in yards, the distance a ball is in the air before it makes contact with the ground.

Total – measured in yards, the total distance a ball travels including hitting the ground and rolling to a complete stop.

Dynamic Loft – measured in degrees, the loft angle of the clubface during impact as it relates to the ground.

POSITIVE ATTACK ANGLE DISADVANTAGES

As with just about every aspect of life there are advantages and disadvantages with information that seems too good to be true. The main advantage of an upward attack angle is that you will generate less ball spin and the ball will travel further, increasing your overall distance. As shown in the previous section, there are major differences in attack angles. The upward attack angle has a huge distance advantage over the downward, no doubt about it.

The main disadvantage of hitting up on the ball is that there is a higher chance of missing the target. The reason for the inaccuracy of upward attack angles is that the ball is in flight for a longer period of time. Longer ball flight time will increase the chance of travelling further away from your target on miss hits such as hooks and slices. If you had a lower attack angle the ball would not be in the air as long and would hit the ground before a hook or slice became worse.

Another reason why the upswing is less accurate is because it usually requires a less lofted driver. The major disadvantage with lower lofted clubs is that they generate less spin. The reason I mention this, because it is more difficult to hit a golf ball straight with a lower lofted clubhead than it is with a higher one. Have you ever noticed how easy it is to hit wedges straight, while the longer irons and woods seem harder? It is much more difficult to slice a lob wedge than a driver. It all has to do with spin. The higher loft a clubhead has, the more spin it generates. The more spin it generates, the higher the ball flight will tend to be.

Unless you are fitted with the correct driver for swinging up on the ball you can be losing distance by creating too much spin. The optimizer swing speed chart shows exactly what launch angle you should try to achieve. If you have a higher swing speed and are playing a higher lofted driver combined with an upward attack angle, your launch angle is going to be off the charts and the ball will spin so much that it will essentially balloon into the air, robbing you and your ego of precious yards. It is essential that you get fitted for a proper lofted driver at a reputable club fitter that is using a launch monitor technology in order to avoid this disappointment.

MOI

A lot of club manufactures throw in complicated terms such as MOI to try to persuade consumers to buy their product. What does MOI mean and does it really affect my distance off the tee? MOI stands for the moment of inertia. It is the clubheads resistance to twisting on off center hits. The higher the MOI (moment of inertia) off the clubhead, the less it will twist during impact with a golf ball. Less twisting of the clubhead will transfer more energy to the ball and make it spring off the clubface more efficiently, producing faster ball speed. Off center hits are defined as anything that isn't on the sweet spot. The sweet spot on a driver is very small, the size of a pencil tip.

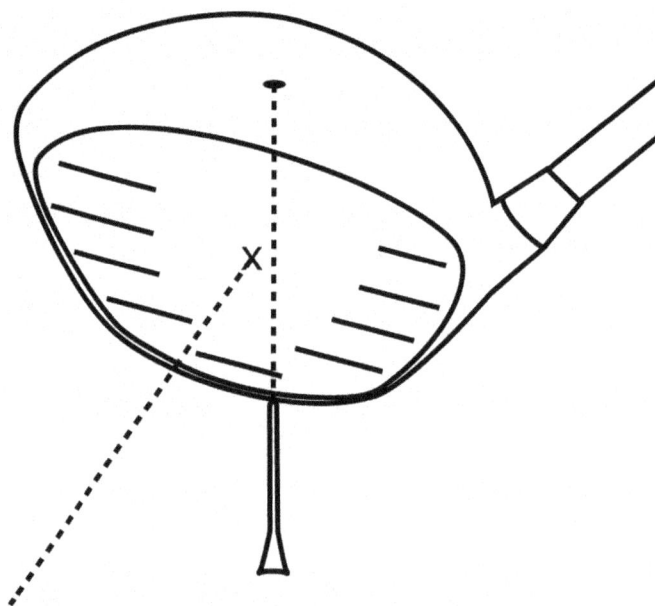

When impact occurs on the sweet spot, the clubhead does not twist.
The tee below the clubhead represents the center of gravity.
Tip: Every driver has different center of gravity depending on the specs of the design.

As you can imagine hitting the sweet spot is very difficult and almost impossible to do consistently unless you are a robot. This is why higher MOI technology has helped the average golfer tremendously. You may only hit the sweet spot once in the entire round if you are lucky. Having a driver with a high MOI will help the club twist less when you don't hit the sweet spot. Drivers that twist less are more forgiving and hit the ball further and straighter.

Off center hits tend to twist the club head around its center of gravity and therefore creates more side spin on the ball. Side spin can reduce your overall yardage significantly and can cause a massive slice or hook. If you are looking for more yardage off the tee and cannot hit the ball on the sweet spot every time, than you definitely need to have a driver with very high MOI. The USGA put a limit on MOI to help make the game competitive and encourage players to rely more on skill rather than equipment. The current limit is 5900 grams per centimeter squared with a tolerance of 100. So in reality the maximum amount of MOI a driver can have is 6000. If you need even more MOI with the driver to boost your confidence off the tee box, you can find drivers that exceed the current USGA limit. However, the majority of manufactures don't creating illegal clubs. The reality is most players won't be playing professional tournaments and USGA rules won't really apply to them. Golf is about having fun. Buy the biggest and highest MOI driver you can find to help you hit the ball further and straighter. A word of advice if you are buying drivers online, make sure they are from reputable sites. There is a major counterfeit problem right now in the golf club manufacturing business. The last thing you want is a fake driver that doesn't perform as well. A little research will go a long way, especially on the course.

Toe Impact   **Heel Impact**

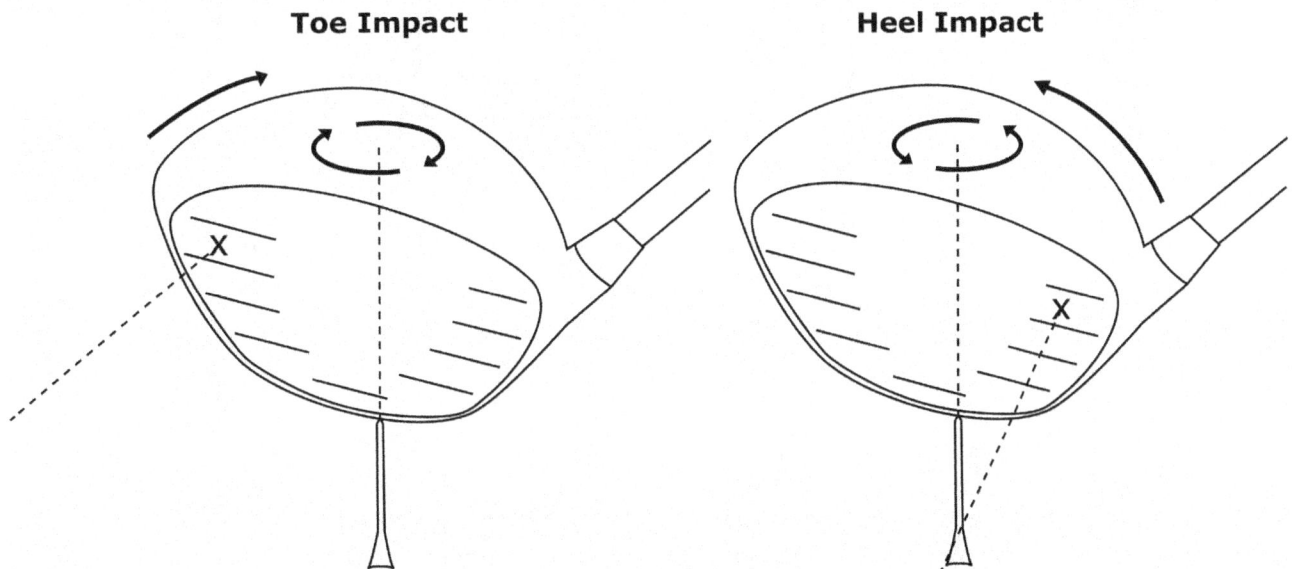

When impact occurs on the toe, the clubhead rotates clockwise around the center of gravity. Visa-Verse, if the impact occurs on the heel, the clubhead will rotate counter clockwise. This causes sides spin to the ball and it will create a draw or fade ball flight.

GEAR EFFECT

You may not notice at first glance, but most modern drivers have slightly curved faces. There is a slight curve from the toe to heel on the driver face. This is called bulge radius. The curve on today's modern driver is very little compared to the olden wooden head drivers. The reason the newer drivers have a flatter face compared to the old ones is because they are bigger and easier to hit straighter.

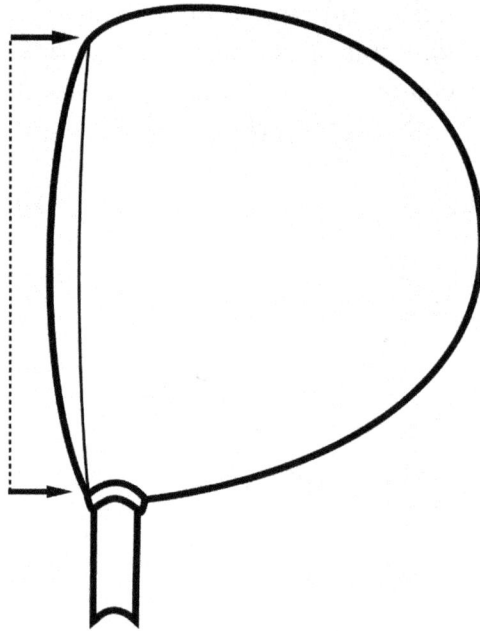

The reason why there is a bulge on the driver is to help you hit the center of the fairway even if you miss the sweet spot. If you do not hit the center or the sweet spot, the club will want to twist away from the center of gravity. Every driver has a center of gravity, some are located in different areas depending on what they are designed for. Some drivers are designed to specifically draw or fade, their center of gravity is more towards the heel or toe rather than being in the middle. This is why having a driver with the highest MOI is vital to reducing your twist off center hits. So where does the bulge come into effect?

It is called the gear effect. If you make contact on the toe of the club face while hitting the ball square towards the target line, the ball will tend to start to the right and draw back towards the fairway. Vice-versa, if you hit the ball near the heel of the club face, the ball will start to the left and fade back into the fairway. Note: this only works if you hit the ball square on impact. If you have an open face on impact you will most likely fade or slice the ball. If you have a closed face on impact you will most likely draw or hook the ball.

So how does this happen? Every driver has a center of gravity. If the driver makes contact with any other place other than the center of gravity, it will want to twist.

Draw

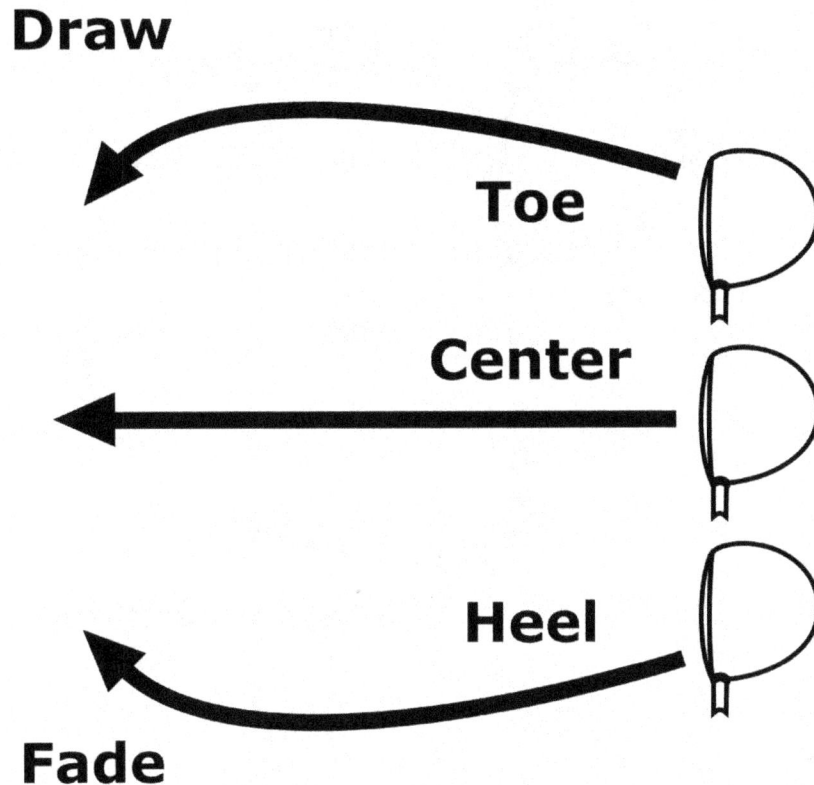

Toe

Center

Heel

Fade

The clubface is square at impact. Toe impact creates a draw, center hit goes straight, and heel impact creates a fade. If you look closely you will also notice that once the ball starts to lose speed as it ends its ball flight marked at the beginning of the arrow, the side spin of the ball becomes more dominant and causes the ball to curve much more.

In this scenario, the ball makes contact with the toe of the clubface. As you can see in the illustration below, the clubhead has no choice but to twist away from the ball due to the sheer force and speed that has been generated. What actually happens is as the club head twists clockwise around the center of gravity, the friction that is created on impact causes the ball to spin counter clockwise. The clubhead moves in a slightly upward direction as it rotates around the center of gravity. The friction causes the ball to follow the path of the clubface as it rotates and creates a hook or draw spin in return.

Imagine the clubhead of the driver and the golf ball had gears on them. The clubhead rotates clockwise around the center of gravity from being hit on the toe. The friction between the golf ball and clubhead act like gears. The ball will create a hook or draw spin because it is following the twist of the club head. This is where the term gear effect comes from.

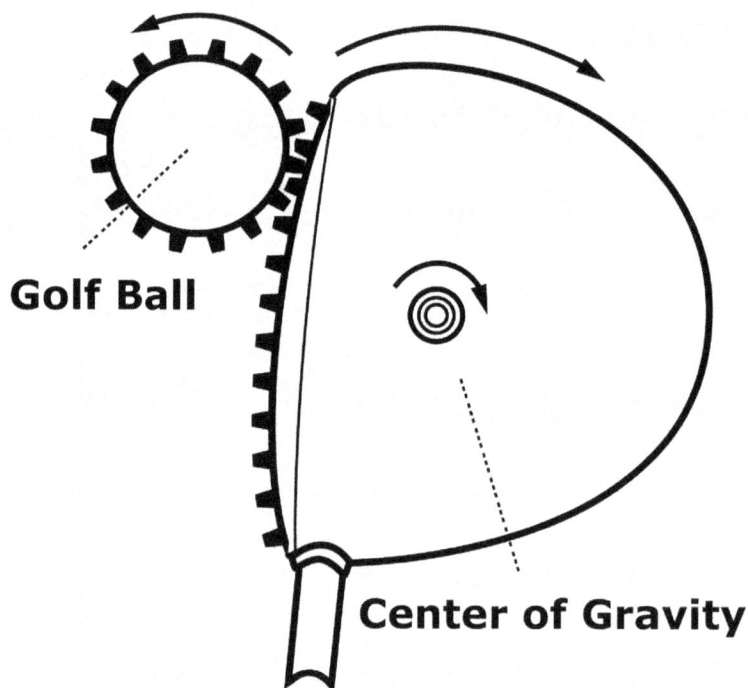

Golf Ball

Center of Gravity

As long as you hit the ball with a square clubface, you can manipulate your flight path without changing your swing or alignment. This is where a solid golf swing comes in handy. You will be tested on a golf course with many dog legs. Don't be afraid. If you have to draw the ball around trees, all you have to do is tee it up closer to the toe. Vice versa, if you have to fade it around to give you a better position in the fairway, just tee it up closer to the heel. This trick only works if you hit the ball square on impact to begin with. If you do not have confidence in your swing to hit it square on a consistent basis, I would not recommend trying this on the course, unless you have practiced it before on the driving range. This works especially well with drivers that have a bigger bulge radius.

Some of the newer drivers have weights that can be removed and switched around to manipulate the center of gravity. This in return manipulates your ball flight. If you are using a weighted driver that has been altered remember, the center of gravity will no long be aligned in the center of the clubhead. You will need to calibrate your ball flights and test the results on the driving range before hitting the course.

SMASH FACTOR

Smash factor is a fairly new term for the golf industry. You may have heard the term recently especially, if you have been near any golf launch monitors. What is smash factor? Simply put, it's the ratio between the ball speed and clubhead speed.

$$\text{Smash Factor} = \frac{\text{Ball Speed}}{\text{Clubhead Speed}}$$

Why on earth would you want to know that? The smash factor will tell how efficient and solid you are actually hitting the ball. It lets you know whether all of that energy you have created with the swing is efficiently being transferred to the ball during impact with the clubhead. Most amateurs tend to focus on increasing their swing speed and in return they suffer yardage loss because they are not hitting the sweet spot consistently. In reality, you should first focus on solid contact which will increase your clubhead speed gradually while making it easier to consistently hit near the center of the clubface for a greater smash factor. Does your drive feel like it is missing something? It probably is. It is missing the sweet spot. If you're not hitting the sweet spot, you are losing potential yards off the tee box. If you only hit 1 out of 10 drives in the sweet spot, you are most likely not benefiting from a higher smash factor. If you want to know what your smash factor is, go to your nearest club fitter and ask to use their launch monitor.

According to Trackman's data, the amateur golfer should strive to have at least a 1.42 smash factor, for the aspiring tour pros the number should be near or greater than 1.47. The highest smash factor rating you can achieve is 1.494 with the driver. The smash factor can also vary depending on the type of golf ball, driver head, shaft type, and club weight. There are many variables to be considered when choosing the right clubs to maximize your smash factor. That is why I recommend visiting a reputable club fitter so they can take the guess work out of the process. Now that you know the smash factor an amateur can easily achieve, are you achieving it? The easiest way to find out whether or not you are reaching your potential is by getting in front of a launch monitor and seeing for yourself. Make sure you double check with the launch monitor operator to see if it's a TrackMan, this will ensure you are receiving the most accurate readings.

If you are not convinced that knowing your smash factor is important, let me prove to you the difference it actually makes. Let's assume you have a 100 mph swing speed with a smash factor of 1.38, the ball speed would equal 138 mph (100 mph x 1.38). If you can increase your ability to hit the sweet spot more often, you can eventually raise your smash factor to 1.47 with the right attitude. A smash factor of 1.47 with your current swing speed of 100 mph, would make a significant jump in ball speed to 147 mph (100 mph x 1.47). This means you would have 9 mph in ball speed increase. As a general rule of thumb, the total distance will increase by 2 yards for every 1 mph of ball speed depending on the conditions. So if you increase your ball speed by 9 mph simply by hitting it closer to the center of the clubface, you will gain 18 yards (9 mph x 2 yards) in total distance. That is a huge improvement that can happen without increasing swing speed. Just imagine hitting it 18 yards further next time you're playing with your buddies just because you are hitting it more efficiently. There are several ways you can increase your smash factor. You can optimize your golf equipment by finding a reputable club fitter. You can also increase your smash factor, by learning new techniques and tips that I will review later in this book. If you are a beginner or going through a major swing change, I would recommend you get comfortable with your swing before getting fitted for a driver. The reason being, your attack angle and swing speed may change over a period of time, especially if you have been working hard on your drills and hitting the gym lately. If your swing changes, you may not be benefiting from your current driver and shaft as much as you could be.

Smash Factor	Swing Speed	Yards
1.38	100 MPH	276
1.47	100 MPH	294

SWEET SPOT

Everyone always talks about the sweet spot, especially me. I am a firm believer in hitting the sweet spot. There is no other feeling like it. Hitting it right in the center and watching the ball just fly away. Wouldn't it be nice to always have that sweet spot feeling? That's exactly what you should be feeling the majority of the time you hit your driver. Many golfers will tell you that it's impossible to hit the sweet spot every time. That may be true. Although with a negative attitude your golf game is going nowhere fast. The best recipe for golf is confidence. The more you have, the better you will play. Confidence is the key to hitting the sweet spot more consistently. You have to believe in yourself. The great Bobby Jones said, the game golf of game is played in the 6 inches between the ears. He is referring to the mental side of the game.

Why is hitting the sweet spot so important? Every time you miss the sweet spot you are preventing yourself from meeting your potential. Let's examine the picture below which shows the clubhead speed in five different clubface areas.

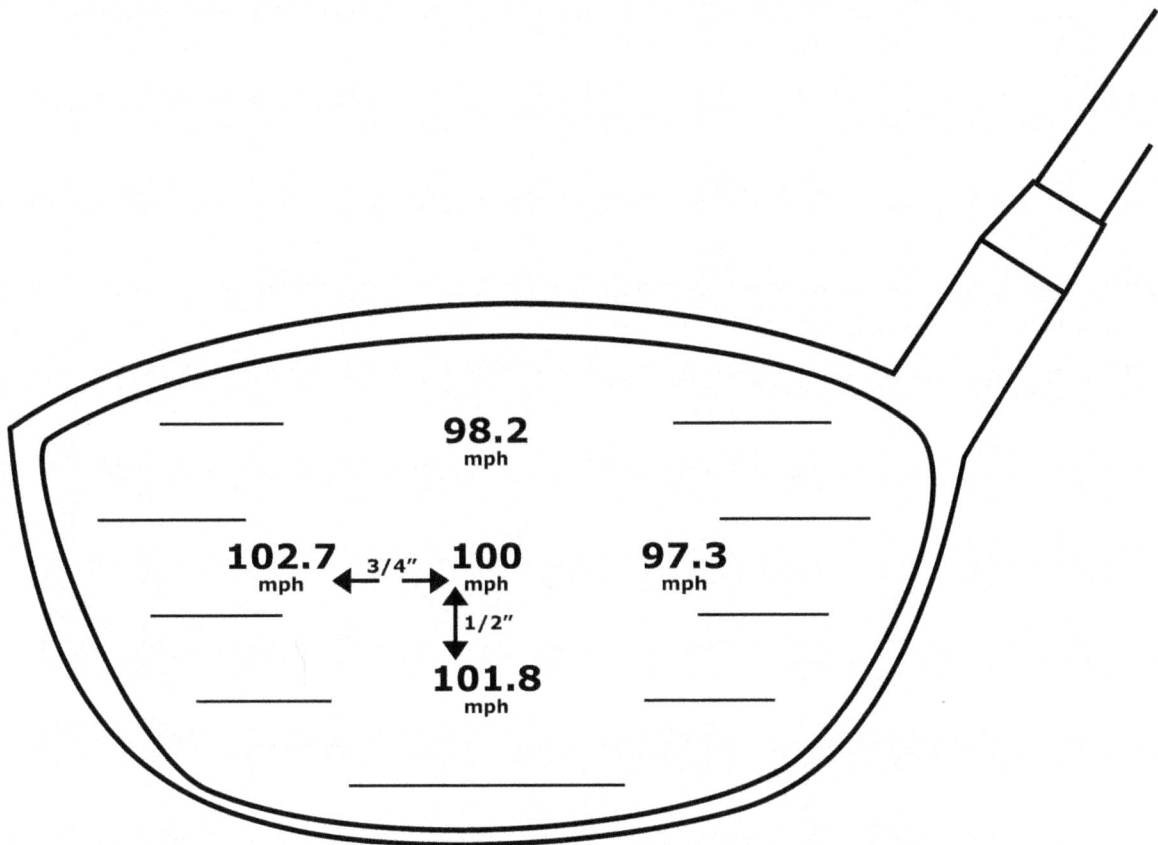

At first glance you will see that the toe of the club actually produces more clubhead speed than the center and heel of the clubface. This happens because the toe of the clubface is further away from the center and heel part of the club. The rotation of the clubhead during the downswing also impacts the speed. The further away from the grip, the faster the clubhead will go. This is the main reason many long drive competitors have much longer shafts than the average driver off the rack. However with longer clubs it is harder to hit straight. So you have to find a length that will balance your particular game, not someone else's.

So does hitting from the toe increase ball speed and overall yardage? This is a tricky question. There is a give and take relationship with golf clubs. Making contact with the toe may increase your clubhead speed, but it will also lower your energy transfer to the ball because it is further away from the center of the sweet spot. This phenomenon is referred to as (C.O.R.) coefficient of restitution. C.O.R. is the measure of energy loss between two colliding objects. C.O.R. measures between 0.00 – 1.00; 0.00 meaning all of the energy has been lost, 1.00 meaning all the energy has been transferred. The best example of all energy lost would be two pieces of tape colliding, they would just stick together so all the energy would be lost and absorbed. The best example of a higher C.O.R. would be when billiard balls collide. The USGA has set a limit on the maximum amount of C.O.R. a golf club can have at 0.83 and most manufacturers strive to be as close as possible. The higher the C.O.R., the more energy transferred from the clubface to the ball. This causes the ball to compress better and bounce off the clubface with more speed.

The key to maximizing distance is hitting your golf ball with the highest amount of C.O.R. possible. The chart below shows the most efficient place to hit the golf ball or the sweet spot of the driver. Remember, some of today's drivers have the ability to change their center of gravity with adjustable settings, making the sweet spot outside of the center. The sweet spot can change from driver to driver. As a general rule of thumb the center of the clubface is still the best place to hit the golf ball.

Impact	Club Speed	C.O.R.
Center	100.0	0.83
3/4" Toe	102.7	0.81
3/4" Heel	97.3	0.81
1/2" High	98.2	0.82
1/2" Low	101.8	0.82

Higher swing speed players are more vulnerable to losing precious yards by missing the sweet spot than slower swing speeds. This is not to say that hitting the sweet spot is not important for slower swing speed players, it is very much so. It is one of the easiest ways to increase distance off the tee box without changing your swing and equipment. If you ask any slower swing speed player, they will tell you they need to pick up as many extra yards as they can. Why are higher swing speed players more sweet spot dependent? Let's say you have a 100 mph swing speed, and you hit 2 drives. One drive connects with the center and the other hits ½" below. The center has a C.O.R. of 0.83 and the lower is 0.82. The carry difference would be approximately 4 yards. As the swing speed increases, the difference between the same 2 drives becomes greater due to the increase in ball speed. If your swing speed decreases however, the difference in yards actually decreases. This is important for higher swing speed players who are consistently missing the sweet spot on a regular basis. You are robbing yourself of many extra yards. If you want to quickly increase distance, buy a driver that has the highest C.O.R. rating you can find. This should also convince you to hit the center of the clubface more often to fully benefit from your drivers potential distance. If you are not confident that you are achieving this goal, please continue reading for great tips and techniques on how to hit the sweet spot more often.

CLIMATE EFFECT

Altitude

The altitude of the golf course also has a major impact on golf ball distance. The higher the elevation, the thinner or less dense the air becomes. The decrease in air density creates less drag resistance on the golf ball during flight. Yes, at higher elevations the golf ball can travel further, but not for everyone. Why? Higher altitudes have less drag resistance on the ball and require more spin to lift the ball in the air. When you see tour pros on TV playing at higher elevation golf courses, the majority of them have been fitted for higher lofted drivers, specific to that certain event. You will need more loft than normal to dramatically increase your distance at high altitudes. Players with high swing speeds have the most success at high altitudes because they generate the most spin. Slower swing players may not always see a distance increase with their drivers unless they already play with higher lofted drivers. On the other hand, many golfers are already dramatically improving their distance, creating sufficient spin to lift the ball in the air. Having properly fitted clubs is the key to generating proper spin and taking advantage of higher altitudes. If you are generating enough spin to create sufficient lift, you may see up to a 10% increase for every 5,000 feet of elevation.

Temperature

The temperature has a significant impact on how the golf balls perform. The majority of golf balls are designed with a specific purpose in mind. Each ball has a different compression ratio. A low compression ball will benefit the slower swing speed player, while a high compression ball will benefit players with faster swing speeds. The general rule of thumb: for every 10 degrees the temperature drops the golf ball will lose 2 to 2.5 yards of distance. When it is very hot outside, the golf ball will tend to compress more efficiently because of the heat, giving you a boost in distance. The exact opposite happens when it is cold outside, especially near freezing. The ball will harden and will not compress as easily, thus preventing you from reaching your full potential for maximum distance. If you have tried to hit a frozen golf ball, you will understand what I am talking about. A frozen golf ball doesn't fly as far, and it hurts like a sting of bees when you mishit. If you are caught playing in freezing temperatures, you can do a few things to help your increase distance. First, keep your golf balls at the proper temperature by storing them in a small pouch with hand warmers, instead of just bare in your golf bag. The golf ball will be nice and warm when you are ready to tee it off, giving you better compression. Second, if possible switch to lower compression golf balls during the cold times because they will spring off the clubface much easier.

Humidity

Humidity is a golfer's worst enemy. It makes the round uncomfortable and makes your skin feel sticky. Humidity feels awful because it makes it harder for your body to evaporate sweat. Instead of drying up, the sweat actually accumulates which can ruin your concentration. There is good news however for golfers when it comes to humidity. Players often assume that when it's very humid the air feels thicker, when in fact the air is lighter. So in reality the ball actually travels further in very high humid air, than in low humidity. Next time you are playing in a hot and humid environment, think of the bright side, it will make your golf ball travel further.

CHAPTER 2

INCREASING CLUBHEAD SPEED - STRETCHES

One of the most neglected parts in the game of golf is stretching. There is this preconceived notion that golfers are not athletes and you don't need to perform any type of stretching before hitting balls. The reality is that golf is a demanding sport on your body and requires supple and flexible muscles to perform at maximum capacity. Many of today's tour pros are amazing athletes. In the future the pros will be longer and leaner, hitting the ball over 400 yards consistently. If you want to get longer off the tee box, you have to take your body condition seriously. One of the most crucial things you can do to help your body is simple stretching. I am not suggesting that you go ahead and take up yoga all of the sudden. I am simply trying to persuade you to start small and work your way up to more advanced techniques. Stretching will not only loosen up your muscles, but it will also enable you to play the game longer with minimal risk of injury. The simple exercises below are designed to be performed before you play a round or hit balls at the driving range. Spend 15 – 30 minutes on stretching before hitting a single ball and you will thank me later. It is also beneficial to stretch at home even if you are not playing golf. This will help keep you feeling loose and ready for the links any time.

Remember not to bounce when doing any of the following stretches. It can tear a muscle and prevent you from playing golf for a few days. If you feel any discomfort, you have reached your limit and should not stretch further to avoid injury. You know your body better than anyone, so make sure you listen to it while performing exercises and stretches.

LOWER BACK STRETCH

This stretch is easy to perform. It is designed to really stretch out your lower back. Many golfers suffer from lower back pain and hopefully this will give you the extra boost that you need.

1) Find a golf cart, tree, post or anything that will support your balance.
2) Grab and hold the object while squatting down with a flat back.
3) Slowly squat down further while pulling yourself away.
4) Hold this position for 15 – 30 seconds depending on your flexibility.
5) Repeat 2 – 5 times, depending on your tightness and schedule.

While performing this exercise, try and make sure you don't bend your knees too much further than your feet. You want to move your lower back away from the post.. Pull away slowly, you will feel the lower back and also hamstrings slowly stretch. The key thought should be to gradually go further away as your muscles begin to relax. If you feel discomfort, you have reached your limit and shouldn't go any further to prevent injury. If feel it is necessary, you can hold this position longer than 30 seconds to really help loosen your back.

HULA HOOP STRETCH

This is one of my favorite stretches. It hits many parts of the body at once to loosen up the kinks. Stretches your back, core, hips and legs. You may hear some bones crack with this one.

1) Place your hands on your hips.
2) Starting clockwise, move your hips around in a small circle, just as if you are starting a hula hoop.
3) Gradually increase the size of the circle.
4) Circle around 10 – 15 times.
5) Repeat in a counter-clockwise direction.

SITTING HIP & BACK STRETCH

This exercise is designed to help stretch your hips and back. This will enable you to really explode your hips during the downswing. To perform powerful drives without injuring your lower back, you need to make sure your hips and lower back are properly warmed up and stretched before hitting any balls.

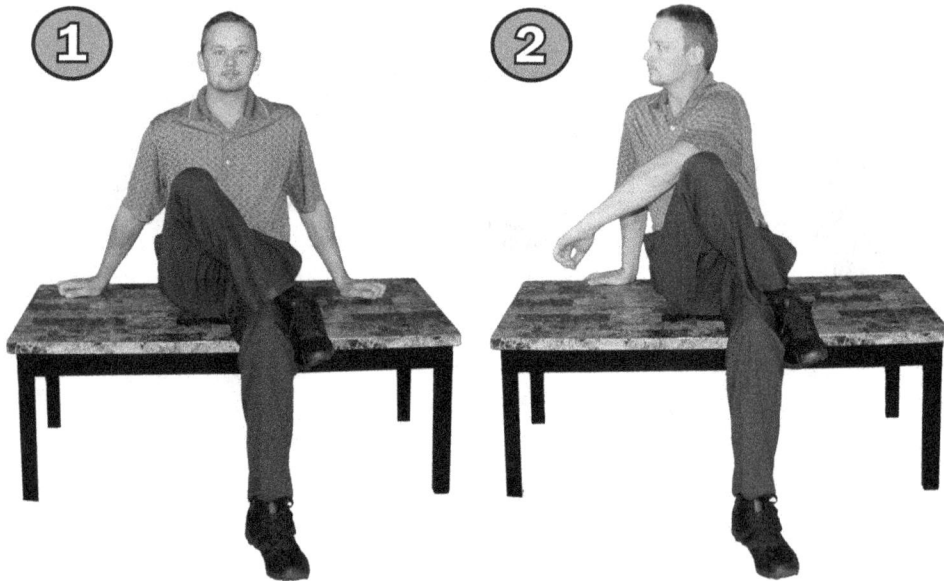

1) Sit on a table, bench or golf cart. Place your right ankle on top of your left thigh.
2) Keeping your spine straight, rotate to your right. Try to use your left shoulder to raise your right knee closer to your body. You may also use your left hand to raise your right knee if you are not as flexible.
3) Hold for 15-30 seconds depending on your flexibility.
4) Switch legs.

You will feel a strong stretch in your right buttocks, hips and lower back.

The buttocks have the largest muscles in the body. It is very important to make sure they are stretched so you can benefit from the power they produce during the downswing.

LEANING HIP & BACK STRETCH

This exercise is very similar to the previous one. It focuses mainly on your back and hips. We want to make sure your hips and back are nice and loose, so you can rotate them properly through the golf swing and prevent injury.

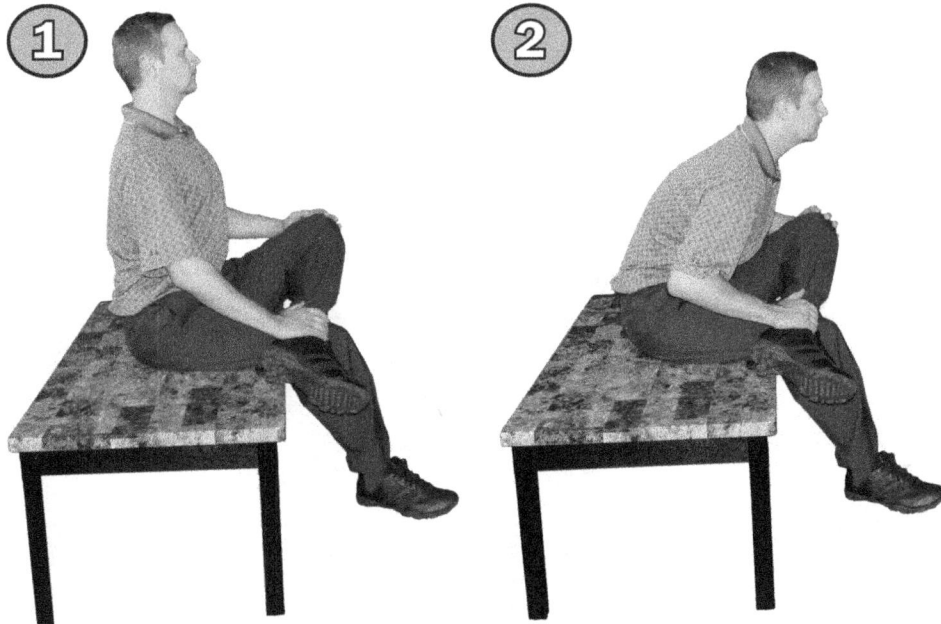

1) Sit on a table, bench, or golf cart. Place your left ankle on top of your right thigh.
2) Keep your spine straight. Slowly lean forward towards your knees.
3) Don't overdue the lean, if you feel discomfort you should stop.
4) Hold position for 15-30 seconds depending on your flexibility.
5) Switch legs.
6) Repeat 2 – 5 times, depending on your tightness and schedule.

You will feel this stretch right away. It really shows how tight your hips can get from lack of exercise and stretching. The tendency with this exercise is to bend your back forward as you can see in image 2. It is very difficult to keep your back straight. Please don't over lean during this exercise, once you feel a stretch in your hips you should stop and focus on relaxing your muscles so they will stretch further.

HAMSTRING & CALF STRETCH

Stretching the hamstrings is very easy. This is a simple yet effective hamstring stretch that also benefits the calf muscles. Every time I perform this stretch, I am amazed by how tight my hamstrings can get without regular maintenance.

1) Put your leg on a table, golf cart or even golf bag with your hands on your hips.
2) While keeping your back straight, gently lean forward.
3) Stop leaning once you feel tightness.
4) Hold 15 – 30 seconds.
5) Switch legs.
6) Repeat 2 – 5 times depending on your tightness and schedule.

It's fascinating how effective this simple stretch really is. The key aspect to remember here is to keep your back as straight as possible. You will notice how tight your hamstrings really are within the first few inches. Once you feel the tightness kick in, stop leaning forward so you don't risk injury. Instead really focus on letting the hamstring loosen so you can benefit even more.

ARM CIRCLE STRETCH

This simple stretch is designed to get blood flowing to your arms and shoulders. You should perform the circles nice and slow to give your shoulders time to adjust. If you have any type of rotator cuff or shoulder injury you should consult your doctor before attempting this stretch as there may be alternative stretches you can perform.

1) With both arms straight, slowly start making small backward circles.
2) Gradually increase the size of the circles until you can't make them any bigger.
3) Perform 10 – 15 circles to complete 1 stretch.

The key to maximizing your overall stretch is to create the circles nice and slow. Don't go too fast just to finish it quickly. Nice and slow, just like the rhythm of your golf swing. After you complete the first 15 backwards circles, you may also want to perform another 15 circles in the forward direction. You know your body best, so use your best judgment.

3 CLUB STRETCH

You will see many tour pros using this stretch. Its basic premise is to swing 3 clubs at once. The additional weight provides the extra stretch you need for all muscle groups involved in the golf swing. This should be the last stretch you perform before hitting balls.

1) Grab 3 clubs. Preferably irons.
2) Address the ball like normal.
3) Starting very slowly, create a quarter backswing and quarter follow through.
4) When you reach your follow through start to swing backwards to your backswing.
5) Repeat and gradually increase to half backswing and half follow through.
6) Repeat and gradually increase to a full backswing and full follow through.
7) Do 10 – 15 swings or until you feel loose.

This is a great exercise and one of my favorites. I never hit a ball without doing this stretch. It really helps loosen up all the kinks you may have missed in your warm up. The key to this exercise is to start very slowly and gradually increase speed as you see fit.

Extra Tip

This drill is only intended for stretching, not for building clubhead speed. There are many people out there that will tell you to use weighted clubs to increase clubhead speed, yet research has shown the extra weight actually slows you down over time.

In order to create more speed, you need to be more flexible and train with more emphasis on stretching and speed. That is why it is recommended that you use lightweight clubs. Make sure to practice the swoosh drill religiously. Lighter clubs are better for increasing clubhead speed because you are actively trying to swing faster instead of harder. Many of the long drive competitors actually focus more on flexibility training. Flexibility training requires you to have more relaxed and supple muscles. Weighted training makes you more tight and slow. Training too much with weights and over doing it can create more scar tissue than actual muscle. If you ever see body builders at the gym, many can't straighten their arms out, which is a direct result of over ripping their muscles, which in return creates overlapping scar tissue. Scar tissue in the muscles makes them less supple and reduces flexibility over time. Instead you should focus more on repetition and let the muscle grow naturally rather than trying to see immediate results. Muscles take a long time to grow naturally, near 2 months if exercised properly. The result will be increasingly flexible and supple muscle that create more clubhead speed than scarred muscles.

As many of you know, the number one killer for power loss is over tightness. The only place you should feel tight is during your backswing near your thigh, hip and oblique muscles. Similar to an elastic band, you are storing all that energy until you release it all on the downswing, creating centrifugal force that will maximize your release to the ball. Centrifugal means moving or directed outward from the center. You want physics to be your friend since it will create much more clubhead speed than your muscles alone could produce.

CHAPTER 3

INCREASING CLUBHEAD SPEED - DRILLS

Increasing clubhead speed is simpler than people realize. There are several drills that I have attached in this chapter that will help you achieve more clubhead speed and one step closer to breaking 300. All of the drills are very easy and should be practiced as often as possible. One of the most unique things about the golf swing is muscle memory. One of most difficult aspects of golf is learning a new technique and actually repeating it during a round. On the course many golfers revert back to their old ways without even knowing it. The reason this happens is muscle memory. It has more influence than your conscious mind realizes because it's controlled by your sub-conscious, which many scientists say is much more powerful. The key to developing a powerful swing is using your sub-conscious effectively. Once you master these clubhead speed increasing drills, it is crucial that you continually practice the drills until they become second nature. You may be surprised that it can take several thousand repetitions before it becomes ingrained in your muscle memory. The bottom line is don't give up and be sure to continually work on your drills whenever possible. I often do many of my drills at home in front of the television during those pesky commercials.

POWER GRIP

The easiest way to increase clubhead speed is to increase your lag. What is lag you ask? In golf it refers to how long you keep the angle between the leading arm and club shaft on the downswing before impact. There are many misconceptions when it comes to the term lag. I want to clarify so you don't become too confused and ruin your entire golf swing in pursuit of the perfect lag. Many amateurs think that you have to hold your lag until the last possible millisecond before releasing the club. That is not true, unless you are a super human who can move his or her arms faster than any of us mere mortals. The average downswing takes less than a second and if you wait too long to release your hinge, you cannot release the clubhead fast enough to square it to the ball. Many golfers will get this idea in their head and not focus on actually hitting the ball solid. There are however several ways to increase your lag naturally so you can focus on the quality of the drive.

Great Lag   **Lost Lag**

One of the easiest ways to increase lag naturally is to use a power grip. It is also referred to as a strong grip. I prefer to use the term "power grip" because it bestows more confidence to the player, resulting in further distance.

Weak Grip   Power Grip

The power grip creates more lag because of the way the hand is situated in the grip. To demonstrate, pick up any club with only your leading arm. First try a weak grip and backswing until your leading arm is parallel to the ground. Then, hinge your wrist. Please be careful when hinging, if you overdue it you may injure your wrist. Take note on the angle of the shaft and your leading arm. Now, try the exact same exercise, this time with the power grip. You should immediately notice the shaft angle is closer to the leading arm. Using the power grip, it feels easier to hinge the club further and with more power. The extra few degrees in the angle you create from using the power grip goes a long way when it comes to increasing your overall clubhead speed. This is one of the easiest ways to increase your lag right from the beginning.

Another benefit of using the power grip is that you don't have to over rotate your spine during the backswing to produce lag. This will greatly help players who have limited mobility. If your body is tight, the power grip will immediately lengthen your backswing without increased rotation. In return you create faster clubhead speed and hit the sweet spot more often with a shorter backswing.

As mentioned before, using the power grip will reduce the dependency on your flexibility. This actually, is good for you. Having a very flexible body is the key to generating amazing clubhead speed. However, some flexible players also suffer from too many moving parts in their swing to compensate for lack of technique. They use their athleticism to square the clubhead at impact. In return, many of these players have a hard time consistently hitting the ball solid. The power grip may be a perfect solution for these players because it reduces the need to rotate your body to get in the same position on the top of the backswing. A backswing with shorter body rotation is much easier to hit solid consistently than a longer one that depends on perfect timing.

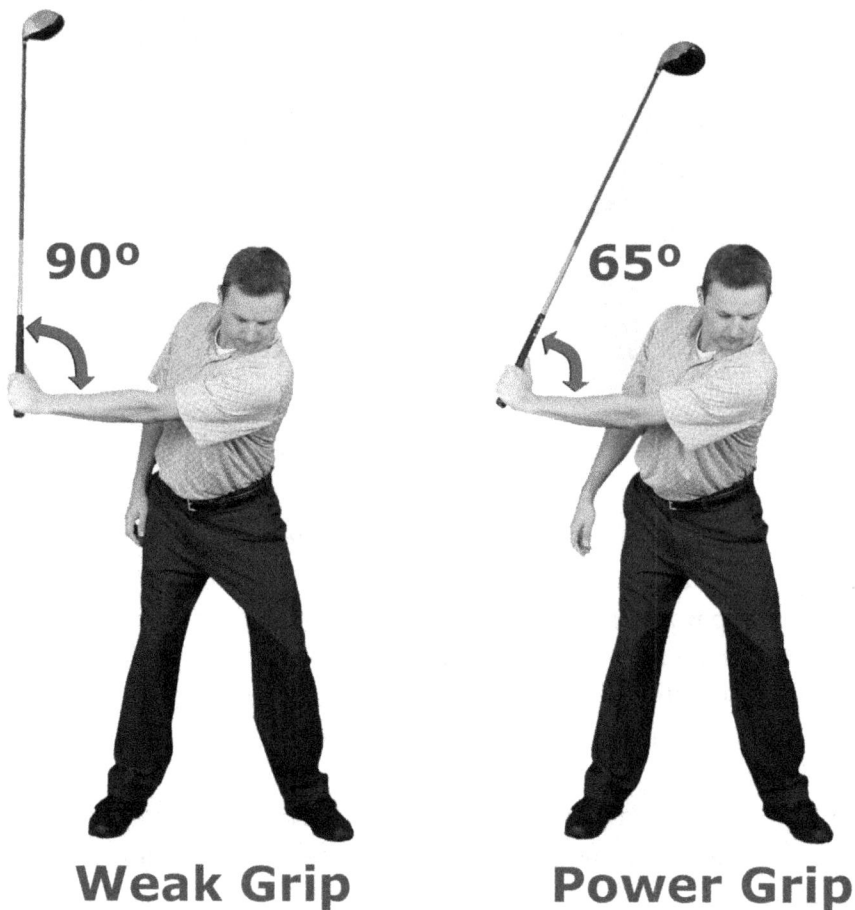

90°

Weak Grip

65°

Power Grip

The great advantage of using the power grip is that you automatically tend to swing from the inside. You may have heard many golf pros say "come from the inside, that's where the power is". It's true, coming from the inside during your downswing actually creates more clubhead speed than coming from the top (out to in). Hitting the ball from the inside tends to start the ball on the right. By implementing a power grip, you will tend to close the clubface on impact more often because you use more of your hands than you would with a weaker grip. By approaching the ball from the inside with more speed coming from your hands, you are creating a very powerful combination. The clubhead speed will naturally increase and produce more of a draw ball flight. A draw ball flight pierces through the air better than a fade ball flight. As a result when the ball lands it will want to bounce and run further than a fade ever will. If you play in wet conditions however, you will benefit more from a fade because it will provide more carry but less roll than a draw. In this case you don't have to change your grip. All you have to do with the power grip is open your stance and play for a power fade.

I must warn you however, not all players will benefit from the power grip. Everyone's body and swing is built a bit different, so some players may benefit more from a weaker grip to increase lag.

POWER GRIP PRESSURE

One of the easiest ways to increase clubhead speed is to have a very light grip. Tension is the number one killer of clubhead speed. If you hold the grip too tight, your muscles are going to be tight. Tight muscles move slower than relaxed muscles. In order to maximize your distance, it is important your wrist and hand muscles are relaxed. The correct grip pressure should be just enough to hold the club in your hand. Think of holding an egg. If you squeeze too tight, the egg will crack. You want to apply enough pressure so it doesn't fall out of your hands. There is a simple drill to check your grip pressure. You can use this anytime you feel you may be gripping too hard.

1) Hold a club up vertically
2) Let it fall out of your hands

You will immediately notice that it doesn't take much pressure to hold a club in your hands. The key is to feel the same light grip pressure throughout the entire golf swing. The lighter the pressure the more lag you will be able to deliver to the impact zone. The more lag, the more distance off the tee.

POWER COIL

A common problem I see is that many golfers hit their wedges with great ball flight, but struggle with longer irons. When attempting to hit the longer irons it becomes more difficult to get the ball in the air because of the lower loft. In many cases the player should be replacing long irons with woods and hybrids, especially if you have a slower swing speed. In most cases the player is not transferring their weight properly. You don't notice the poor weight transfer with the shorter irons because of the higher loft. As you get to the mid and longer irons, the poor weight transfer really begins to affect your ball flight. The bad weight shift also affects the longest club in the bag, the driver. With the driver, your weight transfer needs to be very efficient in order to maximize your potential distance off the tee.

There is an easy drill to make sure you are transferring your weight properly and maximizing your overall power. During this drill, you can pause and really feel your right leg storing all that precious power. You can use any club for this drill, I recommend the driver so you can more easily see the line from the shaft.

You may notice the first time you attempt this drill that it is harder than it looks. Many of your right body muscles are stretching to their absolute max. The key benefit of this drill is that it will increase your spine and lower body flexibility while also helping to strengthen the muscles in those areas. I recommend doing this drill as many times as you can, especially after your warm up stretches. You should strive to do at least 15 repetitions or more a day, even if you are not playing golf. Most people can't play golf everyday so you should do this drill at home in front of the mirror to help with your overall posture. Try to do the repetitions nice and slow. This will help release the tension in your muscles so you can stretch them even further.

1) You will need 3 clubs. Place the 1st club inside your right foot. Place the 2nd club inside your left foot. Take your normal stance and posture. Position the 3rd club in front of your chest/shoulders with your hands crossed while holding the shaft.

2) Start your backswing by rotating your spine. The idea is to rotate the shaft on your chest and line it up with the shaft on the inside of your right foot. If you can rotate past parallel, go ahead and do so but make sure not to lose your posture.

3) Start the downswing and rotate the shaft on your chest towards your left foot. Once you're parallel with the shaft beside your left foot stop and pause.

4) Repeat 10 – 15 times, nice and slowly. Pay close attention to your posture.

While attempting this drill, it is important to feel as if all the power is being stored on your right thigh and right oblique muscles. The muscles will stretch and you will feel a tight sensation. The reason this drills works so efficiently is because you are stretching your key power muscles like an elastic band. The further you train your muscles to stretch, the faster they will come back, just like an elastic band. Doing this exercise also increases the strength in your muscles, especially in the smaller muscle groups that are harder to work out. The smaller muscles are very important in providing stability and strength to the bigger muscles. If you do this drill every day you will notice more power and longer distance off the tee each and every week.

Common Faults

Reverse "C"   ## Building Power

During this drill you may want a friend to take a picture of you or be in front of a mirror as you finish your backswing during step 2. The reason being, if you suffer from a reverse "C" pivot, it will become much clearer to you. A reverse "C" is when your upper body is more tilted and weighted on the left side instead of the right, creating a "C" looking line from the top of your backswing all the way down to your left foot. Performing this drill in front of a mirror will allow you to correct your pivot immediately. Using your right leg as a pivot correctly will ensure that you store the power generated in the backswing correctly.

Advanced Strengthening Tip

Once you become comfortable with this drill you can increase your speed. Increase your speed and try to maintain proper posture and positions. Increasing the speed will enable you to transfer this drill easier to the actual golf swing. If you really want to build more speed alternate with using a single club and several clubs. The difference in weight really confuses the muscles and allows them to react more quickly. Training by alternating heavy and light weights has shown to tremendously increase your overall work out performance.

POWER PIVOT

Storing power in your backswing is a crucial part of hitting the ball further. The easiest way to store power is to use your right leg as a pivot. Many amateurs sway too much and don't store enough of the precious power they are developing during their backswing. Even if you rotate your spine and shoulders properly, failure to store energy with a proper leg pivot will make all that effort go to waste. Similar to the power coil, the power pivot helps ensure that you store your maximum energy potential.

1) Place a club on the ground, you don't need to hit balls for this drill.
2) Address the ball while stepping on the club with the outside of your right foot
3) Slowly swing.
4) Repeat 20 times and increase speed gradually.

This drill may feel very awkward at first. Many don't know how it should feel to properly shift weight using the right leg as a pivot. By placing the club on the outside of your foot, you are able to feel the proper weight shift. Perform this drill as many times as you like, I recommend at least 20 times. After your repetitions, take away the club and try hitting some more balls. You will immediately notice you have more power in your swing with less effort. The power pivot enables you to take advantage of all the energy your body creates during the backswing and helps you to release it more efficiently on the downswing.

In the backswing it is essential to correctly use your right leg as a pivot. Many golfers use their right leg as a pivot but in the wrong way. They transfer the weight to the outside of the foot instead of the inside. If the weight is on the outside, it will promote more swaying and potentially a reverse "C". This makes it harder to transfer the weight to the left side. The correct way to use your pivot is to feel the weight transfer to the inside of your right foot. Using the inside of your foot makes it easier to transfer all the energy stored using your pivot. It also makes it harder to reverse pivot which is a major power killer. The easiest drill you can perform is also the most powerful. The power pivot drill teaches you how to properly shift your weight to the inside of your foot during the backswing. Ensuring a proper weight shift will enable you to hit the ball longer with less effort.

Advanced Tip

Once you become comfortable with this drill you may want to add another club to the mix. Instead of just using your right foot, you can combine both feet. Using two clubs positioned under both sides of your feet you can increase your overall balance. The club on the right foot will enable you to properly pivot on the backswing. The club on the left foot will help you stay within balance on the downswing and follow through. This drill will benefit the players that constantly lose their balance at the end of their swings. Balance is one of the major components to hitting the ball a long way.

POWER BACKSWING

This drill is designed to help you grasp the concept of keeping your left arm straight during your backswing. Having a straight left arm creates the widest arc possible. A straight left arm is necessary to produce efficient power and swing speed. A wider arc also increases the amount of time the clubface is square to the ball during the impact zone. Contrary to popular belief, the left arm does not have to be so straight that it makes your arm stiff and uncomfortable. You may have a little bend in your arm depending on your flexibility and how large your biceps are. This drill is very easy to perform and can be done anywhere. As with any drill, repetition is the key. You don't need a golf club for this drill, but you can use one if you'd like to.

1) Get into address and using your right hand, grab your left wrist just above the hand.
2) While grabbing the left hand, use the right arm to slowly start the backswing until you reach the top.
3) Stop at the top and repeat 20 times.

The right arm should be pushing the left arm away from your body as you begin the pulling of the backswing. Do not push the left arm so hard that it begins to hurt. Just enough pressure is needed to help straighten the left arm.

Depending on your flexibility you may not be able to keep your left arm straight throughout the entire backswing. It is entirely fine not to have your left arm straight. Keeping it as straight as possible without pain is the key to this drill. This exercise is designed to maximize your widest arc possible without injuring or causing pain in your elbow. This drill is very important because it establishes a basic fundamental of keeping your left arm straight throughout the backswing and downswing. Looking at all of the long hitters on tour, most of them keep their left arm straight throughout the backswing and downswing. Therefore this drill is designed to increase the consistency and power by creating the widest arc possible. The wider the arc in your backswing, the greater the tendency will be to square up with the clubhead during the impact zone. Hitting the ball square and on the sweet spot is crucial to maximizing your distance.

A wider arc is the key to more clubhead speed. Think of it this way. Pretend you are a helicopter. If your rotor blades are too short, you will not generate enough speed to create lift to get off the ground. Therefore you need long enough rotor blades to increase your speed so you can achieve the proper lift to fly away. You see, the longer the rotor blades, the faster they go, and the more lift they create. The same goes for your golf swing. The wider your arc, the faster the clubhead will travel. That is one of the secrets of long hitters. You can also buy a longer shaft for your driver to create even more speed. The problem with longer shafts is that they are harder to hit straight. The key is to balance the length of shaft with your game. Professional club fitters can easily help you with that.

POWER HINGE

The power grip gives you the basic foundation to increase your lag. It won't however, do you any good if you lose the majority of the lag you acquired by releasing the clubhead too early in the downswing, otherwise known as casting. One of the biggest ways to lose that precious lag and power is to release to clubhead from the top of the backswing instead of near the bottom.

The answer to this problem is to continue a slight hinge of the wrist on the start of the downswing. In other words, just as you are finishing your backswing, continue hinging until you start the downswing. In return you will create even more lag than before. Many long drive professionals use this technique to maximize their distance. Once you perfect this technique and start seeing results, you will notice that all this extra power is created effortlessly. It feels easy once you become comfortable because you are creating a substantial amount of centrifugal force.

1) Start your backswing slowly until you reach near the top.
2) Transition slowly into the downswing while still hinging your wrists.
3) Hold the wrist hinge all the way until the impact zone.
4) Repeat 30 times at half speed before hitting any balls.

This drill may feel strange at first, but if you follow through and do enough repetitions, you will naturally store all the energy and lag until you are ready to hit the ball. The secret to this drill is to hold the lag until the impact zone. I recommend performing at least 30 reps at half speed so you don't overdo it and injure your wrists. When you are ready to hit balls you will notice how easy it is to do so. The ball will travel much further with less effort and it will all be thanks to the power of lag.

Benefit of Power Hinge Drill

Doing this drill correctly automatically puts you in a better impact position. You don't want the clubhead too far in front of your hands at impact. The reason for this is that the clubhead travels faster just behind the hands or near the bottom of the swing arc. Once the clubhead goes past the bottom of the arc, it starts to decrease in speed. This drill will help you create more lag, put you into a better impact position and increase your distance.

CHAPTER 4

INCREASING SMASH FACTOR

In order to hit the ball further, you will have to learn how to increase your smash factor. The smash factor determines how efficiently you are transferring energy from the clubhead to the ball during impact. This is much easier than people realize. You can increase your smash factor easily by focusing on several key components. In this chapter I will address some basic principles that I feel are important in increasing your energy transfer efficiency.

A key point to remember when performing any drills is balance. Swing within yourself. If you tend to try too hard, you probably are robbing yourself of distance. Instead focus on staying in balance. Many of the long drivers of the ball make it look so easy. That is because they stay in balance instead of falling back or forward in there follow through. Learn to swing within you yourself first and then gradually increase speed.

IMPACT ZONE

With today's technological advancements, the drivers are designed for maximum forgiveness. Even on off center hits, the ball will travel fairly far. Thanks to advancements in M.O.I (moment of inertia), the clubhead doesn't twist as much as it used to. The key to hitting it longer and straighter is to make contact with the sweet spot more often. If you hit the ball on the toe or heel, the drive can lose a tremendous amount of carry and distance. This loss of carry will start at about 10 yards and can even add up to 100 yards depending on how bad the mis-hit was to begin with. To maximize your overall distance you need to figure out your impact zone pattern. To achieve this, you need to figure out exactly where the ball makes contact with the clubface of the driver.

1) Attach impact tape or use the dry erase marker to completely cover the clubface. Please do not use permanent marker as it may not come off.
2) Take a swing and hit the ball. Use your pre-shot routine just like you would on the course.
3) Hit several balls and record the results. Remember to use a new piece of impact tape or fresh coat of dry erase marker with each and every shot.
4) Analyze the results.

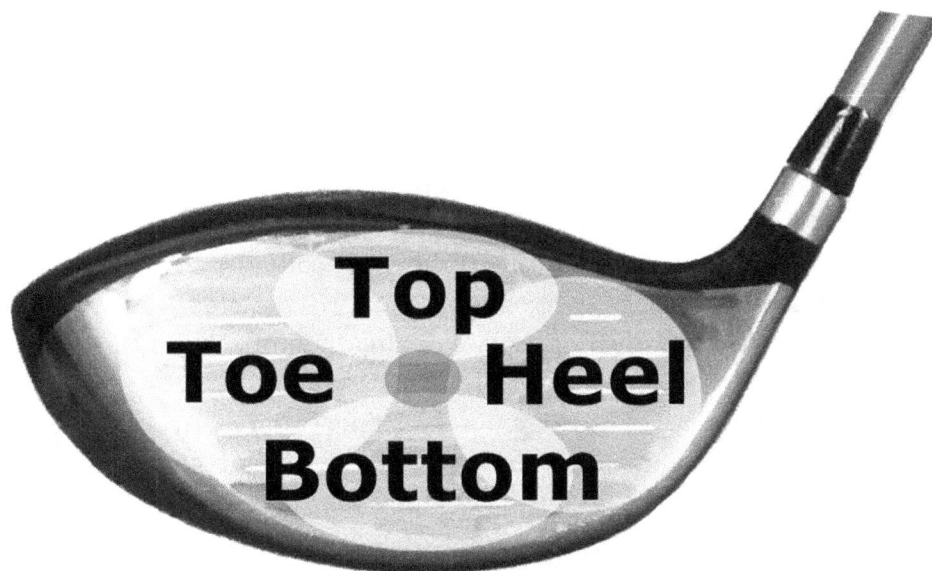

Results	Solution
Hitting the **center** of the clubface more often.	Perfect. Don't adjust ball position.
Hitting the **toe** of the clubface more often.	Slightly move ball position closer.
Hitting the **heel** of the clubface more often	Slightly move ball position further.
Hitting the **top** of the clubface more often.	Adjust the tee slightly lower.
Hitting the **bottom** of the clubface more often.	Adjust the tee slightly higher.

The best way to approach the solution is to set the tee higher or lower and ball further or close until you start hitting the sweet spot more often. The reason being, your mind will want to go back to old habits, so you have to intentionally set up the ball position before you start your swing. The impact zone test will surprise many of you. Seeing where you actually make contact with the ball will shift your paradigm. It enables you to fix the ball position to maximize your distance off the tee without making major changes to your golf swing.

WIDER TAKEAWAY

The easiest way to increase distance is to ensure square impact on the sweet spot more consistently. To accomplish this, the clubface needs to be square during the impact zone. This sounds much easier than it actually is. Most amateurs don't hit the ball solid for one reason; the club face is rarely or never square on impact. The golf ball only compresses on the clubface for a fraction of a second, so you have to be confident the clubhead is square to the ball to maximize distance potential. To achieve greater success with squaring the clubhead, you have to increase the amount of time the clubface is traveling square during the impact zone.

An easy way to increase the length of the clubface being square during the impact zone is to widen the swing arc in your backswing. To achieve this you need to start with a wider takeaway. Widening your takeaway is fairly easy and has helped me to hit the driver square more often. Below is an easy drill to widen your takeaway.

1) Tee a ball and place another tee 3 feet away from the target line.
2) Address the ball and try to hit the second tee in your takeaway. If you can't manage to hit it then try to get near it.
3) Repeat 20 times or until it becomes comfortable.

If you can't hit the second tee, that is perfectly fine since your arc will make the clubhead rise up naturally. The most important thing is that your hands are extending a bit more than usual. A different method is to use your shoulders to move the club while having the feeling as if your hands are trying to extend the club as far as possible until the shaft is pointing towards the second tee 3 feet away. Personally I prefer to use the second method because it gives me a slightly wider arc and in return creates more of a power coil. While using the hands to extend the club during the takeaway, don't try to extend so far that it becomes uncomfortable. That would just make your arms too stiff and cause less flexibility when trying to set into the backswing. You don't want to feel any pain during drill. If you do feel pain from trying to hit the second tee, it may be placed a bit too far.

That's all there is to it. Repeat this drill 20 times at the range before hitting balls. Another tip is to perform this drill slowly and methodically. You want a smooth takeaway. Take your time performing this drill as you don't want to start creating bad habits right off the bat.

Having a good take away is crucial to your overall swing. Creating this wider arc at the beginning of your swing will automatically tell your brain on the downswing to imitate the clubhead near the same path you started. If done correctly, your downswing will be more consistently square with the club face and produce higher and longer ball flights.

SWOOSH DRILL

The swoosh drill is one of the most basic and important drills out there. Most amateurs release the powerful energy created by their swing and club shaft much too early, resulting in a massive power loss. This is mainly done by casting the club, in other words hinging or cocking the wrists on the down swing much too soon. When you watch tour professionals they usually don't hinge or cock the club on the downswing until the shaft is parallel to the ground. The reason the tour pros wait until the last second is to release all of that stored energy at impact, rather than before it even reaches the ball. If you cast or release the downswing too early, all of that centrifugal energy will be released before it even comes close to the ball. As a result the club head will already be decreasing in speed by the time it makes contact with the ball. On top of it all, your body is wasting precious energy in trying to compensate by swinging past the ball too hard and making you lose balance.

To make a self-diagnosis as to whether or not you are wasting any energy before your clubhead even makes contact with the ball, you should implement the swoosh drill into your practice routine. This easy drill will help you realize where you are releasing all of that powerful energy. You will also realize how important this drill is when attempting to consistently repeat the same release of the club head. It will help create maximum clubhead speed during the impact zone.

When you first begin this drill, it may be hard to tell at first where the sound is made, but with practice you will be able to pin point the origins of the swoosh sound.

1) Take your driver and flip it upside down. Take your normal grip near the end of the shaft where the club head is.
2) Swing and listen. You will notice right away that the shaft makes a swoosh sound near the ball. The key to this drill is to figure out when the swoosh sound is made. Listen carefully. If it is made before the ball, you are releasing the energy much too early. If it is made 2 feet away from the ball, you are releasing the energy too late. If the swoosh sound is made within inches of the ball, you are correctly releasing. The magic release point is just after the ball within a couple of inches.
3) Repeat 10 - 30 times until you are consistently swooshing near the ball.

After finished with this drill, go ahead and flip the driver back to its original direction and take some practice swings. Remember to always use your pre-shot routine when swinging any club, even if it is for practice. This might feel awkward at first after doing the swoosh drill. The swing weight is going to be a little heavy at first. Don't worry, after a couple of swings you will regain your comfort. Take your practice swing and just like before concentrate on where the swoosh sound is being made. The same as before, you want the swoosh sound to be made right after the ball. Now go ahead and hit some balls.

This drill may seem easy and primitive, but don't be fooled. The swoosh drill is used on a daily basis even by successful tour pros. Before you even waste any energy hitting full shots on the range, the swoosh drill should be used to make sure you are releasing the energy at the right spot to maximize your distance potential. People are not machines and they do tend to fall back on old habits. It is crucial to constantly practice basic drills so as not to let your sub-conscious bring back old swing habits. This drill should be used on a daily basis and be part of your foundation arsenal.

THROW THE BALL DRILL

The throw the ball drill is one of my favorite drills and has helped me tremendously in the search for more distance. Many golfers have struggled with over rotating their shoulders and spine too fast on the downswing in order to hit the ball further. Players feel the need to unwind their upper body as fast as they can in order to hit it harder. This only robs the player of precious power during the impact of the golf ball. The major problem with rotating the upper body too fast is that the hands can never catch up in time. As a result, the clubhead is released too far ahead of the ball. The maximum clubhead speed is several feet in front of the ball rather than inches where you want to be. You also cannot fully unhinge or release all the lag created until after the ball, simply because it has no room to catch up. The shoulders turn too much and the right arm becomes trapped and can't clear through the hips. This is a common power loss problem that can be easily fixed just by applying this simple drill. This will help ensure that you maximize total distance with your current abilities. Performing this drill correctly will also ensure that you are in the proper impact position to help you compress the golf ball even more.

All you will need for this drill is a golf club and a golf ball.

1) Hold the grip of the clubhead with your left arm straight in front you while in your usual address position.
2) Whiling holding the golf ball in your right hand, initiate the backswing with the right arm only.
3) Start the downswing and throw the ball down on the ground towards the target line. Remember to keep you left arm straight and quiet.
4) Perform 10 - 30 repetitions

Are you throwing the ball high in the air? If you are, that is an indication that you are releasing too late and not shifting your weight properly. The point of this drill is to throw the ball to the ground and watch it bounce a couple of feet towards the target line. You may want to experiment with the distance on the first bounce. Everyone's body is built different, so the exact distance the ball should be thrown may be differ. One thing is for sure, if you throw the ball before the impact zone you may be releasing too early.

Once you become comfortable with this drill you should notice immediate results. It will be awkward at first. Getting used to this new sensation will help you swing with more clubhead speed. I recommend performing this drill every time you play, just to remind yourself not to over rotate your upper body. This drill teaches you how to properly release the golf ball without trying to overpower the swing. If you watch the tour pros on television, you will notice many of them hit 300 yards without even trying. The tour players create effortless power because they know the secrets of lag and how to release it properly.

Another Key Benefit

When performing this drill you will notice that the left hip clears naturally. Many players use the right hip to drive into the ball. As a result, their hips rotated too much and their hands have nowhere to go and essentially become trapped on the downswing. If you become trapped on the downswing, meaning the right elbow hits the right hip, your body will want to compensate. This will add more swing flaws and make it that much harder to square the clubface on impact. Using this drill will help you to naturally rotate your hips so you can focus on hitting the ball.

DOWNSWING SEQUENCE

One of the hardest parts of the golf swing is figuring out the proper sequence on the downswing. The first instinct is to initiate the downswing using their arms and try to swing as hard as possible. This is counter-productive in creating swing speed. It also results in a loss of balance and a lower chance of hitting the ball straight unless you have amazing hand eye coordination. The pros make their downswing seem so easy. The reason being, they use bigger muscles to initiate the downswing. Their arms and wrists are the end of the downswing sequence, not first. You should start the downswing by first slowly rotating your hips. Once the hips start moving, the spine starts to stretch to the limit and retract similar to an elastic band. When the club becomes parallel to the ground, the arms and wrists should start to straighten. Following this sequence ensure you are creating maximum swing speed possible. Understanding this sequence may be hard to comprehend. To help you understand easier, I use the rail road train sequence example.

Train #1 – Lower Body/Hips (Slow Speed 20 mph)
Train #2 – Spine/Shoulder (Medium Speed 70 mph)
Train #2 – Arms/Wrists (Very Fast Speed up to 150 mph)

There are 3 trains. Each train is designed to go at a different speed. Train #1 is the slowest train, travels at 20 mph, it carries very heavy cargo. Train #2 travels at medium speed, around 70 mph, faster than train #1 because it carries medium weight cargo. Train #3 is the fastest. It is designed for high speeds of up to 150 mph. It carries only passengers so it has a very light weight to pull and uses magnets instead of conventional railway. All 3 trains need to make it to the station a mile away near the same time.

Top of Backswing

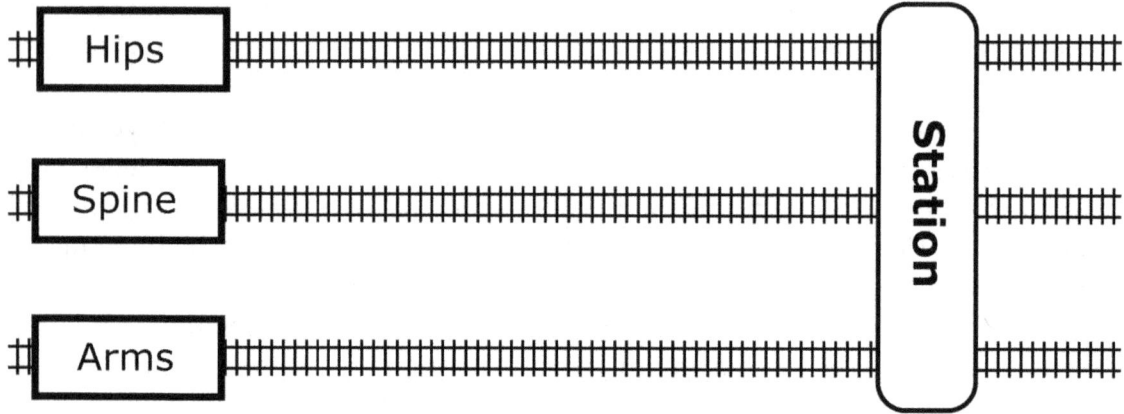

Hips	Station
Spine	
Arms	

Start of Downswing

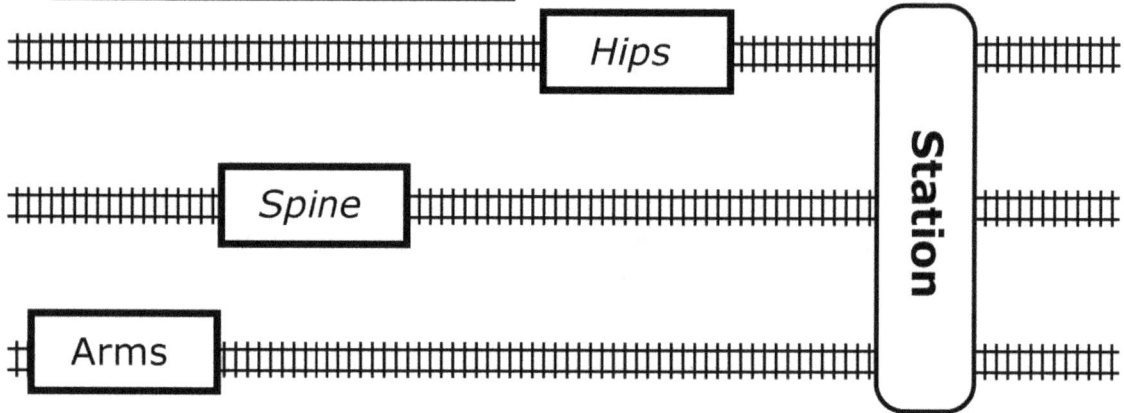

Hips	Station
Spine	
Arms	

Impact

| Hips |
| Spine |
| Arms |

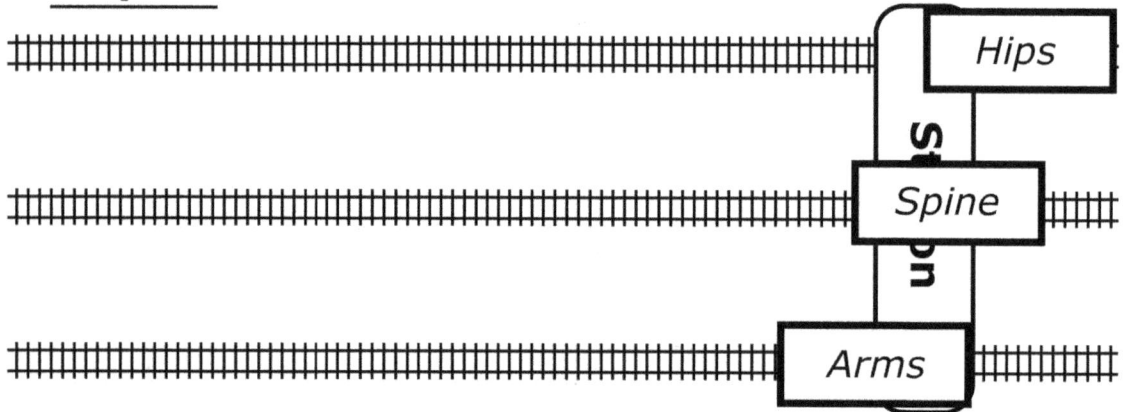

Hips = Slow, Spine = Medium, Arms = Fast

In order for all 3 trains to arrive near the same time, the slowest train needs to leave ahead of the other two trains. Once train #1 has a good head start, train #2 can leave and start catching up. Once both the slower trains have left, the high speed train #3 has to wait a while before it can begin its departure. Train #1 has reached its distance checkpoint and train #2 has reached its distance checkpoint. It is finally for the high speed train #3 to depart and catch up with the other 2 trains. Since train #3 is so fast, it only takes it a fraction of the time. When the 3 trains finally arrive at the station, they all arrive near the same time. Arriving near the same time ensures the maximum efficiency for the workers at the station.

The downswing isn't complicated if you think of the 3 trains. You can practice this at home in the mirror. The hips (train #1) go first. The spine/shoulder (train #2) naturally will follow with the resistance you are creating by the stretching your hip muscles. The arms/wrists (train #3) are only to be initiated once you reach the "L" position is reached. Practice the power hinge drill if you are problems with this part. The "L" position lets the shaft become parallel to the ground on the downswing without using the hands to release the club. When you reach this point the safety is off and you are free to swing at full power with your arms/wrists. If you initiate the hips first, the release of the clubhead will come naturally due to the centrifugal force being created.

CHAPTER 5

INCREASING CLUBHEAD SPEED - WORKOUTS

To increase distance you need to increase clubhead speed. To increase clubhead speed you have to improve strength and flexibility in the key power muscles. The forearms, shoulders, core, lower & mid back, hips, gluteus & legs all are power muscles in the golf swing. Research has shown that using lighter rather than heavier weights and focusing more on quickness increases clubhead speed the most. Keep that in mind when creating a workout regimen for yourself.

Power Muscles

Forearms ——

—— Shoulders

Core ——

—— Lower & Mid Back

—— Hips

Glutes & Legs ——

FOREARM STRENGTH - STRESS BALL

The stress ball is one of the easiest workouts you can do to increase clubhead speed. This workout is very easy and convenient because you can do repetitions at work or at home. The best part is that it does four different jobs at the same time. First, it builds muscle in the hands and wrists. Second, it gives you more stamina so you can play longer. Third, it helps prevent future hand and wrist injuries. Fourth, it relieves your stress. Having strong wrists is important in the golf swing. The hands and wrists are the final piece to fire before making impact with the golf ball. You want to make sure they are strong and healthy. Many golfers don't realize the amount of force that is created on impact with a golf ball, especially if you are hitting into the ground. The stronger your wrists become, the more lag you will be able to store on the downswing and explode on impact.

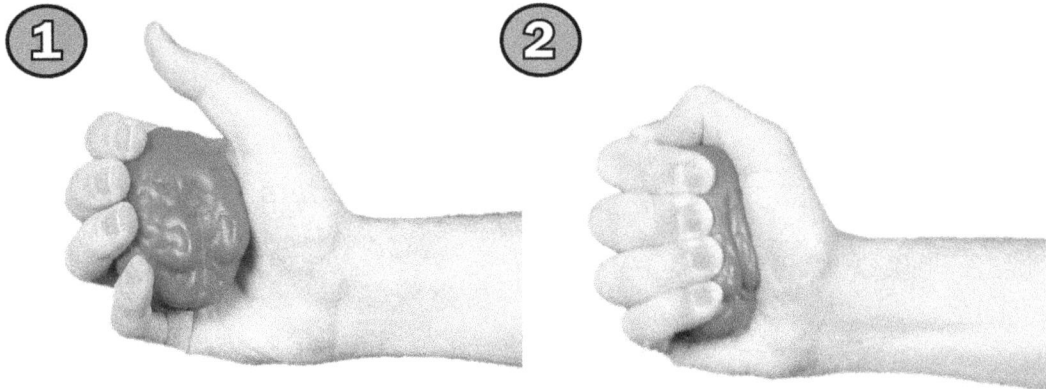

1) Grab a stress ball.
2) Squeeze stress ball than let go.
3) Continue squeezing for 1 – 5 minutes or until you feel a slight burn.

I prefer to squeeze the ball quickly instead of slowly. My reasoning behind this is that you are training your body to build speed and strength. Many of the long drive hitters train with speed and quickness in mind instead of lifting heavy weights slowly. You want to fire up your fast twitch muscles instead of the slow ones. If you constantly train with heavy weights and move slowly, how can you expect your body to increase speed? If you train your body with speed and quickness, then you can expect your body to perform faster.

When you first start this exercise you will feel a deep burn in your wrists. When the burn starts it's time to stop and take a break. Start with just a few repetitions per day and increase as it becomes more comfortable. As your wrists get stronger, so will your golf swing.

SHOULDER STRENGTH – ROTATOR CUFF

If you want to hit the ball further, you have to make sure your shoulders can absorb the extra impact. The shoulder muscle group is very unique. The shoulder is the most complicated joint in the body. It also happens to be a common area for golf injuries. Having strong shoulders will enable you to play the game longer and with more power. Many people are surprised at how well they start playing after a couple months of shoulder strengthening. The key to strengthening your shoulders is to target many of the muscle groups. This shoulder exercise targets the smaller rotator cuff muscles that are typically neglected. Many people only work out larger muscles and wonder why they still sustain injuries in the shoulder. The key to hitting the golf ball longer is to make sure both the bigger and smaller muscle groups are flexible and strong. Strengthening the smaller muscle groups will help your body tremendously. This rotator cuff exercise is designed to help keep your shoulders strong and healthy in order to increase clubhead speed.

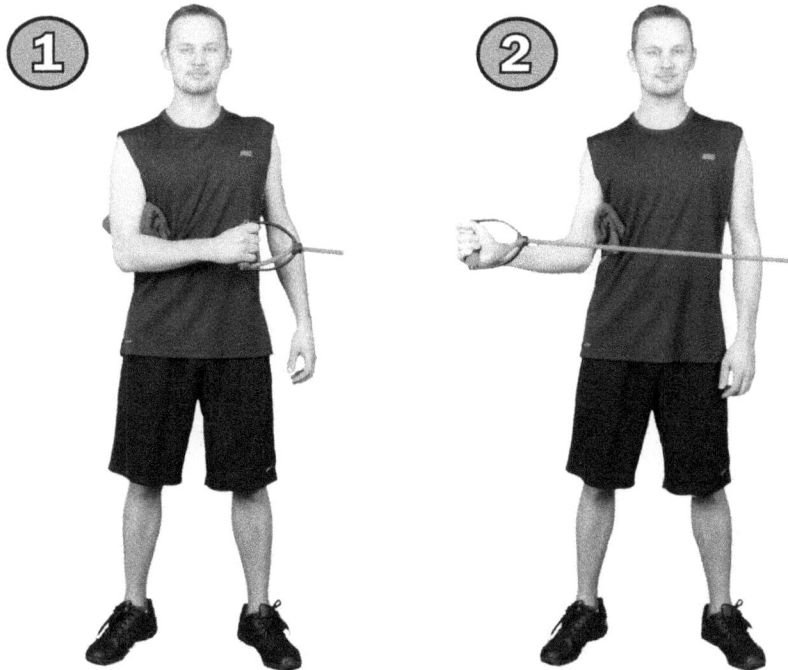

1) Fold a towel under your armpit and grab a light weight resistance band.
2) Rotate your shoulder internally and externally than switch hands.
3) 12-20 repetitions with 3-5 sets for each internal and external shoulder rotation.

The key with this exercise is to use a light resistance band because you are working out smaller muscle groups. Using heavy resistance may pull and tear the smaller muscles. Many people neglect the smaller muscles in the shoulder. Once you start performing this exercise, do not overdue it. Start slow and work your way up. Your shoulder will tell you if it can handle any extra resistance. It may take several months to really build up the smaller muscles in the shoulders. Let me tell you, it is well worth the wait. You will feel much stronger. The golf swing will more effortless than before. Strengthening this muscle group is one of the easiest ways to increasing clubhead speed. The arms connect to the shoulder, so if the shoulder is weak, you will increase your chance of injury once you start improving your clubhead speed.

CORE STRENGTH – OBLIQUES

One of the keys to building a powerful swing is having a strong core. Your core connects your upper and lower body. It is also a main source for torque in the golf swing. The stronger your core is, the more clubhead speed that will naturally occur in the downswing. One of my favorite core workouts is using a resistance band. I prefer to work out with resistance bands over weights the majority of the time. The resistance bands offer a major advantage over weights. Unlike weights, the bands provide resistance both ways of the workout. Weights don't work as well when gravity takes over. In my experience my muscles also feel more supple with the use of bands, instead of the bulk that can occur when using heavy weights.

This workout incorporates many muscle groups including your core, lower back, and hips. Using these muscle groups also helps you with the balance of the golf swing, since are standing straight.

1) Loop the resistance band over a sturdy post. Hold both ends of the band with your hands. Setup up with a golf address in mind.
2) Start stretching the band away from the post until you reach about a foot away from you. Return to your original position.
3) Perform 3-5 sets of 12-20 repetitions each.

This exercise is great for all golfers who want to learn how to explode into the golf ball. Doing this exercise correctly will benefit your golf swing in several ways. First you will stretch one of the key areas that affect your backswing. In time your backswing will be more flexible. This exercise also targets the oblique's, which will help you rotate your upper body with more power and ease, creating a better shoulder/spine turn. Those of you with lower back problems will benefit from this exercise greatly because it also targets the low back. Using the resistance bands makes your body struggle hard to stay balanced. Having great balance in the golf swing is crucial to delivering power consistently. Lastly, this is a great way to learn how to use your right leg as a pivot. Many golfers don't pivot properly and sway in the golf swing. To be able to hit the ball far, you have to learn how to store the powerful energy in your right hip. When performing this exercise it is beneficial to stand in front of a mirror. You can see if you are swaying while returning the band to its original starting position. You will feel natural resistance in your right hip. The key concept is to think of it like the start of your backswing. You are storing the energy in your right hip and oblique. Once your hands are back in the starting position, explode into your left side. Remember not to sway during this exercise. Doing this workout 3 times a week will result in more clubhead speed very quickly.

Extra Tip

Do you find that straightening your arms during this exercise is uncomfortable? You can perform this drill with the elbows bent more. This will also let you rotate smoother and faster and have less chance of injuring your arms. It is up to your preference whether you want to use straight arms or bent arms while rotating.

LOWER BACK STRENGTH - SUPERMAN

The lower back is very important in the golf swing. Keeping it healthy will not only enable you to play longer, but hit the ball further as well. Your lower back takes a beating on a daily basis. The back constantly works hard during your hundreds of golf swings on the course and driving range. Add on top of that, your everyday activities such as sitting, lifting, slouching, etc. The lower back seems to be one of the most neglected parts of the body when it comes to exercise. Most people will strengthen their biceps and abs at the gym to look better in the mirror while the back suffers. This exercise, called the Superman, helps strengthen your back so you can continue doing the activities you love. It is very easy and can be done anywhere. I recommend doing this exercise right before you turn in for the night. If you do this exercise in the morning especially if you already have a weak back, you will feel sore. If you perform the Superman exercise right before you go to bed, you can sleep away any soreness that may occur.

1) Lie down on your stomach and position both your hands in front of you like Superman.
2) Keeping your feet together, lift your legs and arms slightly higher until you feel tension.
3) Hold this position as long as you can until discomfort sets in.

When first performing this exercise you will notice it is very difficult to hold the position. That is a clear indicator of how much your back is being neglected. You have to strengthen your lower back tremendously if you want to take advantage of speed and power during the golf swing. As you progress and become more able to perform this exercise, you will want to hold the position longer. You may perform this exercise several times a week. As the weeks progress you should notice your lower back feeling better and stronger. This exercise will not only benefit your golf swing but also your day to day life.

HIP & LEG STRENGTH – LUNGE & TWIST

One of the biggest power generators in your body are your hips. Your hips are crucial to increasing clubhead speed in order to break 300. Having strong and flexible hip muscles as well as lower back and leg muscles will help you drive the ball further than ever before. Do you ever notice how the tour pros manage to hit the ball so far and make it look easy? They understand the power of the hips and use it to their advantage. The downswing is initiated with the hips first to allow your core to stretch to the max just like an elastic band. The key to power is to stretch those muscles even more with your hips. In order to achieve more distance you will need to strengthen your hips and the connecting muscle groups. This exercise is great because it hits many muscle groups at once so you can get the most out of your work out session.

1) Grab a medicine ball
2) Lunge forward with right leg.
3) Twist towards right leg and hold for 5 seconds.
4) Go back to standing position, switch legs and repeat 12-20 times

This may be very hard to do at first. Start off with a lower weight medicine ball and work your way up as balancing becomes easier. The key with the exercise is to twist without losing your balance.

HIP STRENGTH – HIP ROTATION

Strengthening the hip muscles is the key to longer drives and effortless power. Your hips turn internally and externally. When you start your backswing your right hip is actually externally rotating. On the downswing your right hips goes from an external to an internal rotation. The golf swing requires that your hips have the flexibility to rotate both directions. The stronger and more flexible your hips become the easier your hips will be able to rotate in the backswing, downswing and follow through. Keeping your hips strong and flexible is one of the most important aspects of hitting the ball long. This exercise strengthens your hips by rotating both internally and externally.

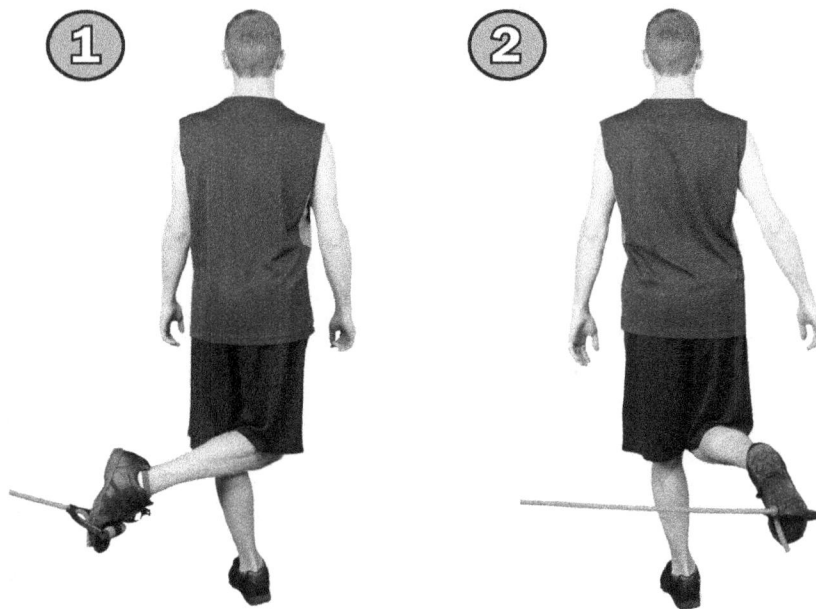

#1 External Hip Position, #2 Internal Hip Position

1) Attach a resistance band to your foot and lift up.
2) Stretch the resistance band with your foot and rotate the hip internally with 12 reps.
3) Move band to the other side and rotate the hip externally with 12 reps
4) Switch feet and repeat.

To make this exercise easier, you can rest your knee on a bench for support. I prefer to stand so I can work on my balance at the same time. I normally perform 3 sets of 12 repetitions each. I switch feet between each set to give my right hip a break as I start working on my left side.

CHAPTER 6

CLUB FITTING

The easiest way to increase your distance off the tee is to get professionally fitted by a reputable club fitter. Don't just go to any club fitter. Do your research. Ask what type of equipment they use to determine the best fit. You want to make sure that your club fitter has a launch monitor. Without a launch monitor, the club fitter won't be able to give you precise measurements such as distance, clubhead speed, ball speed, launch angle, spin rate, attack angle, and dynamic loft. All of these measurements are crucial in figuring out how to maximize your distance potential. If the club fitter is not using a launch monitor, they are basically fitting you blind and selling you a driver right off the rack. You will gain the most distance just by getting a driver that fits you properly. Once you get custom fitted you will never purchase another club off the rack again. There are a few key aspects of club fitting you may want to be familiar with. Knowing more about your club specs will give you the ability to maximize your playing ability and let the club fitter know what you are interested in.

THE GRIP

The grip should be one of the first parts of the club you look at. It is the easiest part of the golf club to switch if you have to. Today's grips come in many styles and colors. Choosing a color that relaxes you is essential. You want to feel relaxed on the tee box. So make sure you pick a color that helps you go to that happy place. Don't buy a color because it matches your car. Pick a color that you like to look at.

The next part of the grip is the texture. You want the grip to feel very comfortable in your hands. Depending on your playing conditions, you may need a special grip that suits you. If you tend to play in the rain you may want grips design specifically for wet conditions.

The last part of the grip you want to look at is the width. Believe it or not the width plays a tremendous role in creating clubhead speed. The thicker the grip, the slower you will release the clubhead near impact. The slower your release, the slower your overall clubhead speed will be. A wider grip will also have a tendency to favor a fade ball flight. The reason being, a thicker grip takes longer to release so the clubhead will still be open during impact. If, on the other hand, you have a thinner grip, you will be able to release the clubhead quicker. The thinner grip allows you to unhinge faster and will favor more of a draw ball flight. The draw ball flight comes from the faster release because the clubface will tend to close more often during the impact zone than a thicker grip would. You can use the grip thickness to your advantage. If you have a problem with slicing, a thinner grip may be part of your solution. Vice versa, if you want to get rid of your hooks, a thicker grip will certainly help you with that. The thinner grip may give you more clubhead speed or maybe not. It all depends on the player and their ability to swing with thinner and thicker grips.

Ultimately, it all really comes down to player preference. Feeling comfortable with your grip is crucial. If you don't like the grip you are playing now, you will never have the confidence you need to drive a ball down the fairway. Don't be afraid to try out a few grips until you become confident. You can always replace the grips if you don't like them.

THE SHAFT

The shaft may be the most complicated aspect of a golf club. It doesn't have to be. You don't need to know every miniscule detail about the shaft as long as it's properly fit to your swing. Some aspects of the shaft you may want to know are the type, flex, kick point, weight, and length.

The type of shaft is important. The majority of shafts these days are made from graphite instead of steel. Graphite is much lighter and creates more clubhead speed than steel. It is also more expensive. You will notice when shopping for a new shaft, the lightest shafts tend to be the most expensive. The lighter the shaft, the more research and development typically goes into creating the product. That is one of the reasons some light shafts cost a small fortune. In order to provide consistently great performance a lot of time and technology goes into creating state of the art graphite shafts. Although there would be no point of having an ultra light shaft if you could never hit it straight.

Graphite has come a long way since first being introduced in the golf market. The graphite shafts for drivers come in thousands of models in today's market place. Choosing the correct one may be difficult. That is why it is essential you try out several models and see the results on the launch monitor before even thinking about settling down with a shaft. Certain model shafts may feel great but are they performing well too? Many of the club fitters have electronic shaft analyzers attached to clubs that will help automatically determine several models from a database. This narrows the search quite efficiently so you can focus your testing on 2-3 models instead of going through them all.

The shaft flex is also very important to consider. The shaft flex comes in L, R, S, and XS. The problem is that the industry does not regulate the actual shaft flex. This means that one company's S flex could actually be compared to a different company's R flex. Don't just buy a shaft and expect it to be you're desired of flex. Test the shafts first and make sure it is what you are looking for. Most club fitters will determine your flex by your swing speed and tempo. The higher your swing speed, the stiffer your flex should be. The majority of golfers are playing with shafts that are too stiff for their swing speeds. The shaft flex is there to help you get the most out of the club, so don't let your ego get in the way of maximizing your distance. You can also manipulate the ball flight with different shaft flexes.

Every shaft has a kick point also known as a bend point. The 3 kick points are low, mid and high. If you want a lower ball flight because you tend to play into the wind a high kick point may benefit you more than a low kick point. High kick points tend to have a lower ball flight. Low kick points tend to haves higher ball flights. Mid kick points tend to be more in between.
The shafts also have torque ratings. The torque rating tells you how much the shaft is going to twist during the swing. The lower the torque, the stiffer it will feel. This really comes down to

preference. If you want your shaft to feel soft, you will want a higher torque rating. You also have to keep in mind your feel preference. A shaft that feels good will make you more confident on the golf course.

The length of the club is one of the easiest ways to gain distance. Choosing the proper length of a shaft can be a double edged sword, however. The longer your shaft is, the more clubhead speed you will produce. The shorter the shaft is, the slower your swing speed will be. However, the longer the shaft, the harder it becomes to hit straight. This is where the double edge comes into effect. Before you get fit for a driver, you have to make a decision about what your priorities are. Do you want to hit the ball longer and miss more fairways? Or do you want to hit more fairways but be shorter? You need to ask yourself these questions. What will your game benefit more from? Hitting more fairways or being closer to the pin on your second shot? If you are a professional long drive competitor, the longer the shaft the better. Long drive athletes have extremely long shafts. The normal driver off the rack is 45 inches long. Meanwhile the long drive clubs are sometimes more than 55 inches long. The long drive competitions recently implemented a rule to limit the length of the club to 50 inches. The problem with the long drive competitors is rarely any of them contend in professional golf tournaments. Professional long drivers focus on distance and as a result accuracy is harder to maintain. If the long drivers could hit it straight consistently they would have a huge advantage over the other tour pros. Most tour pros use a 45 inch driver because they are more accurate and they can count on them when it matters most. So in the end it all comes down to what kind of golfer you are. Are you a long driver or a contender?

THE CLUBHEAD

The clubhead is the base of the club. It has come a long way since the wooden days. Today's clubheads look cooler, bigger, more forgiving and more advanced than ever before. Why not take advantage of it? If you are playing with a 10 year old driver it may be time to get a new one. I am not saying to buy the newest model released every year. Seems like these days the manufacturers release a new line of drivers every six months. What I am saying is that in 10 years the driver has gone through dozens of advancements that will benefit you more than your current one. You might as well look and see the difference for yourself. When you are ready to buy a new driver make sure you bring your old one as a reference. You don't want to just take my word for it, you want to see proof. The club fitter will ask you to take several drives with your old driver and display the results. Once the data is recorded, it's time to test out the new models. You won't believe the difference. With the same exact swing you will see astonishing improvements. The real magic begins when the club fitter starts handing you different shafts to try and tweaks your club.

The look of the clubhead plays a vital role. Like in fashion everyone has their own individual style. The same applies to golf. Believe it or not, the way your club looks will affect your performance. Golf is a mental game. If you are playing with a driver you can't stand looking at, than you are in a world of trouble. Not only will you be telling yourself how hideous this driver looks, you will also tend to over tighten your grip from disgust. We all know by now that one of the worst things you can do to your golf swing is to tighten up. Tension kills speed, and in return diminishes your ability to hit the ball longer. If on the other hand you had a nice looking driver that you are proud to play with, you will feel happier and more relaxed. Your grip will naturally loosen and bomb the drive down the fairway. The appearance of your driver is one of the keys to increasing distance and breaking 300. Next time you're in the market for a new driver, do yourself a favor and find a clubhead you like to look at.

The appearance of the clubhead is very important but so is the sound of it. Hearing a driver can either be exceedingly pleasant or terribly disturbing. Some drivers are so loud they will burst your ear drums. Do you ever hear drives on the golf course that you just can't stand? Those annoying driver sounds that make you lose your focus. You can't control the sound of other drivers, but you can certainly control your own. The sound of a driver is intentionally very unique between models. It is a way of trade marking for the manufacturers. If you play enough golf you will be able determine the exact model of a driver a player just by the sound it makes. Many manufacturers do this on purpose. Similar to music, people like and dislike certain types. Driver sounds may also feel good to you or not so good.

Sound is a very powerful sense and it releases very potent brain signals. When you hear sounds you like, the brain sends signals to make you feel good. The most notable signals are with dopamine receptors. Dopamine is released into the brain when you feel happy. It is the sensation everyone is always chasing. This phenomenon in the brain is very powerful and makes you feel good. You can have your own personal dose of dopamine just by finding a driver that sounds good to you. Every time you hit that driver, you will feel good. The better you feel the looser you will become. The looser you become the more flexible you are. This all equates to longer drives. A good trick to help you find the right sounding driver is to bring your golf balls when you are being fit. Many golf balls sound and perform different when you try other drivers and you want to make sure that you are testing the correct type of ball with your new driver.

Another very important aspect of a driver is how it feels. Every golfer has a certain type of feel they prefer. Many players haven't tried enough drivers to know exactly what feel they are looking for. That is where the club fitting process comes in. You have the ability to try several models. Many times I see people who are already determined to buy a specific brand because their favorite tour pro is using them. That is fine, but it may not be best fit if you are looking to improve distance. You can't discriminate against drivers because you prefer certain logos. The key is to try out several drivers without worrying about the brand name and the massive marketing campaigns that follow. Find a driver that feels good for you. It will do wonders for your game. If you have a driver that looks cool but feels awful, you won't be very confident when you approach the tee box. Being uncertain and feeling horrible about your ability to hit a good shot is not the frame of mind you want to be in. Instead, find a clubhead that feels good. Even if you mis-hit the shot, it will still feel good. Having that constant comfortable feeling with your clubs is very important. The better you feel the more confident you become. Before you know it, you will get in the zone more often than you're used to. All thanks to your new clubhead that is boosting your confidence.

TECHNOLOGY

The technology on today's driver is outstanding. When you compare first generation metal woods to the newest generation, they are literally decades apart in research and development. The introduction of titanium drivers helped revolutionize the game of golf. Lighter and stronger metal allows for more clubhead speed and further distance. The titanium metal also helped make the clubhead larger and more forgiving on off center hits. In the process of creating a more efficient clubhead, the distance increased dramatically over the years. As a result, the golf courses are being made to play longer than ever before. It is easier now than ever to hit the ball over 300 yards. Don't be surprised if in the coming years, average drives on tour increase are over 400 yards on a consistent basis.

The new composite head drivers available today offer a combination of titanium, tungsten and carbon fiber. The purpose of using carbon fiber is that it makes the clubhead even lighter and improves performance. They place the tungsten in certain points of the clubhead to increase forgiveness and stability. The MOI is at its limits with today's driver already. The majority of drivers in today's market have legal limit of 5900 grams per centimeter squared with a tolerance of 100. The legal size of the clubhead today is 460 CC. Many of the drivers available today already reach these limits. As a result, the manufacturers are focusing their energy on designing a clubhead that is even more forgiving by strategically experimenting with different types of material to improve performance even more. Not only do the newest drivers offer incredible technology, they are also adjustable. Many of today's drivers come with adjustable weight and shafts to enable you to manipulate your ball flight. You can change the center of gravity of your clubhead by simply moving the weights around to your preference. You can even rotate the shaft now and change your face angle, lie and loft of the driver. The benefit of these new technologies, you don't have to worry about changing your golf swing to produce a different ball flight. Instead just change the clubhead setting. This new invention has made the driver more user friendly. Instead of buying multiple drivers to play certain conditions, you can save your money and buy only one clubhead that can be adjusted to your changing needs. It's like have having several drivers for the price of one.

LOFT

The loft of the driver is very important to increase your maximum distance. The problem is many of the golfers today are playing with drivers right off the rack. Most drivers off the rack have lofts of 9.5 degrees. As a result many recreational golfers are playing with not enough loft to reach their distance potential. As a good guide, you need a swing speed of 95 mph or greater to fully take advantage of a 9.5 degree driver. If you have a slower speed you are going to lose precious yards by playing a 9.5 degree driver. The problem that I see is the player's ego gets in the way. Recreational golfers see the tour pros playing 9.5 degree drivers and that is what they buy off the rack. Instead of just buying the 9.5 driver that is sitting nice and pretty in the golf store, talk to your local club fitter and try them out for yourself. When you are having your club fitting session, don't be afraid to try out the 9.5 degree driver to see what kind of numbers you will post.

After you get your fix, try out the other lofts the professional club fitter recommends based on your current swing speed. The launch monitor numbers don't lie, they have no reason too. The launch monitor is not biased to anyone so you know you can trust it. If you have a slower speed you will tend to benefit more from higher lofts. Vice versa if you have a higher swing speed you will benefit more from lower loft. There is a magic loft degree that is right for you and your current swing.

Why is loft so important? The loft will determine how much spin you can put on the ball. The problem is many different players will produce difference spin rpm with the exact same club. Not every player has the same swing, so the spin from the same loft varies from player to player. That is why you want to go see a club fitter and have them use launch monitors so you can determine what works best for you. If you are creating too much spin with your current driver, the ball may be ballooning into the air and losing yards. Instead of spinning towards the moon, your ball should be traveling more towards the target. The same is true if you don't produce enough spin. The ball won't travel far enough because it doesn't have enough spin to stay in the air. Spin creates lift. The lift is what keeps the ball in the air and from hitting the ground too early.

You can also essentially change your loft by your attack angle on impact. It is called the dynamic loft. It is measured in degrees, the loft angle of the clubface during impact as it relates to the ground. If you want to create more loft you simply hit the ball on more of a positive attach angle. If however you need a lower loft, you only need to decrease your attack angle. However I don't recommend changing your swing to suit your needs unless you are very good ball striker. I would suggest learning to hit one swing first before venturing on to any more swing thoughts. You will just ruin your game and any hope of hitting the ball further.

GOLF BALLS

The technology has come a long way in the golf industry. The golf ball is the biggest benefactor by far. The distance in golf has mostly been increased due to the advanced research and development into the ball. Today's golf balls can spin less with the drivers and spin more with the wedges. On the market available today there are one, two, three, four and even five piece balls. The one piece balls are not commonly used as playing balls rather driving range balls. It is made with low quality in mind intended for beginners and practicing. Although inexpensive many of these balls are durable. Traditionally the one piece balls have a very soft feel on impact.

The two piece ball is the most used ball on a day to day basis because it provides durability and maximum distance. Usually a two piece ball is made with a hard plastic solid core. This ball gives the most distance out of any ball because of the high energy acrylic resin. It is also cover with a cut proof material. The two piece balls are generally referred to as hard balls and used by many of the long drive competitors. Another advantage the two piece ball is its high rolling distance which makes it the most popular golf ball for the average golfer.

Three piece golf balls are wound balls with solid rubber centers, covered with yards of elastic windings. The windings are covered with a molded cover made from durable Surlyn or liquid balata. Three piece balls are softer and create more spin because of the windings. It has the advantage of being more controllable than a two piece ball. If you prefer to be able to spin for control, than a three piece golf ball is for you.

Manufacturers have recently created four and five piece golf ball. The advantage of using four and five piece balls, the manufactures have been able to create less spin with the driver and more spin with the wedges, the best of both worlds. There has been much skepticism around these new balls. The best way to see if they are for you, take them out for a test drive.

All golf balls have a compression ratio. You may even see the number on your golf ball. Today's golf balls have compression ratios of 80, 90 or 100. There is a big misconception about how the compression ratio actually works. Most people believe the higher then compression, the further the distance will be. Yet there are many published studies done with a golf swing machine that indicate no such truth. The studies have shown that the 80, 90 and 100 compression balls built in the same manner actually land within couple yards of each other. What does this mean? It is more important to look at the model of ball rather than the compression ratio. The compression ratio is more related to feel. Do you like to hit a soft or harder ball? However when you play in freezing temperature, having a lower compression ball is beneficial because it will help spring off the clubface better. When a golf ball comes close to freezing it loses its elasticity. Once that happens the golf ball won't perform to its full potential. Playing a lower compression ball during colder climates will help you gain distance.

With new advancements come more choices. There are hundreds of golf balls available in today's market place. They key to maximizing distance is to find a ball that fits right for you. The expensive tour balls may not be suited for you. There is only one way to find out. Try them out on a launch monitor and see the results for you. There is no point in guessing your actual distance if you can have precise yardage reading instantly using a launch monitor. When you are playing out on the course, the conditions always change. The temperature can be different. The ground may be wetter or firmer. The wind could affect the ball flight. There are so many variables to put into account it becomes very difficult to compare golf ball results on the course. It becomes difficult to know what ball is optimizing distance for you. The benefit of a launch monitor, you can just relax knowing the conditions are the same. When trying out different model of golf balls, it is important you hit enough balls. Always take the average of 5-10 swings. Unless you can mimic the exact swing over again with the similar launch angle, having an average will give you a better indication of which ball is right for you.

FINAL WORDS

I wrote this book to help regular golfers with their pursuit of breaking 300 yards down the fairway. Growing up playing golf religiously, I always fell short of obtaining the 300 yard distance marker. I read all the golf tips I could find on the television and in books. Some worked and others didn't. I finally realized there wasn't a quick fix to hitting the ball further. In order to hit the ball further I would have to dedicate hours of practice time and work hard to achieve my goals.

The first aspect I worked on was my golf game. Learning new drills won't help you unless you are working on basic fundamentals. The basic fundamentals that I feel are crucial to increasing distance are listed in this book. I started with basic drills that laid the foundation for creating power in my golf swing. These drills are basic power generation techniques that have worked for many players including myself. Having basic drills to always fall back on is crucial. As you may know, it is very difficult to continue playing well throughout your golfing career. Only a few professionals have ever succeeded in careers that last decades. The main reason for their success is their ability to come back to the basics regularly. Anytime a golfer experiences a bad day or perhaps a season that isn't going well, the player should always go back to the basics. It is much easier to practice the basics instead of trying to reinvent your swing with new drills.

The second aspect I worked on was strength and flexibility. It is difficult to generate more clubhead speed unless you are strengthening your body. Your body is the key to the golf swing. You need to make sure it is healthy and flexible. Most people believe you need to work out 3-4 days a week in order to improve your swing. This simply is not true. Many pros only work out 2 days a week. They get away with 2 days a week because they do the correct exercises and let the body heal the rest of the time. If you can set up a schedule and work hard 2 days a week for just 30 minutes, you will notice huge improvements in your distance in no time. The key before any work out, especially as your body ages, is to stretch. Spend as much time stretching as you do on strengthening exercises. Stretch before and after. Creating and maintaining flexible muscles will help you hit the ball further off the tee box. As I started strengthening my body, the golf swing became easier for me. Distance just came naturally and effortlessly.

I also have to mention, golf drills and strengthening exercises are not any good if you don't do them correctly. Most of you have heard of the term practice makes perfect. In golf, the term is perfect practice makes perfect. The key to the golf swing is muscle memory. You don't want to think about anything when you swing because it will ruin your game. Too many thoughts in your head at address will make you lose confidence and second guess your ability to hit the ball. The key is to use muscle memory in your favor. It takes thousands of repetitions to store muscle memory into your swing. One of the main reasons it's so hard to learn a new technique in golf is that old habits from years ago return. Just imagine the countless number of repetitions you did with your old golf swing. So when you try to learn something new, it becomes difficult. The key to learning a new technique is to work hard over an extended period of time. If you start a new drill, don't just give up, keep working hard and eventually it will pay off. Just make sure you are performing the correct drill for your swing or it will all be for nothing.

There is no better feeling than hitting your driver on the sweet spot and watching it fly down the middle of the fairway 300 yards away. I hope this book will help you in your journey towards hitting the golf ball 300 yards long and straight for many years to come.

REFERENCES

TrackMan Optimizing Charts
http://www.trackman.dk/download/newsletter/newsletter2.pdf
http://www.trackman.dk/download/newsletter/newsletter3.pdf
http://www.trackman.dk/download/newsletter/newsletter7.pdf

ONLINE GOLF LESSONS

Do you need help with your golf swing? If so, please visit my website www.breaking300.com where I allow my students to upload their golf swing via the internet. Within 24-48 hours a professional video is created highlighting your online lesson. You will see your golf swing on video with commentary just like the pros do. The benefit of having an online golf lesson, you don't have to travel and you can view it any time at the comfort of your own home.

Your swing will be professionally reviewed to optimize distance with the driver. The golf swing doesn't have to be complicated. One of the best ways to learn is to actually see what you are doing on video. The ability to see your golf swing on video has revolutionized the way golf is being taught. Instead of an instructor just telling you the faults of the swing, they can show you. On my website, you will be provided with easy to learn concepts that relate to your golf swing.

I believe in adapting my teaching style to the individual player. Not everyone comprehends information the same, so it's crucial to not overwhelm the student and provide simple yet affect techniques.

I focus more on dynamics than anything else. If you have a strong foundation the rest of the swing will naturally come into place with minor tweaks. Understand the basic swing dynamics is the key to effortless golf. Golf doesn't have to be hard. If you learn the basics correctly you will have more fun, shoot lower rounds, and hit the ball further than you ever thought possible.

www.Breaking300.com

LONDON LEAF PUBLISHING

If you enjoyed this book, please visit our publisher's website for more titles and updated news.

www.LondonLeafPublishing.com

ABOUT THE AUTHOR

Fil Falcon is an author and publisher. He is dedicated to sharing his passions and to growing the game of golf. He graduated Professional Golfers Career College with honors and received a specialized associate's degree in professional golf management.

www.ingramcontent.com/pod-product-compliance
Lightning Source LLC
Chambersburg PA
CBHW081516040426

42447CB00013B/3240